HELLO, WEST INDIES

Hello, West Indies

Morris Weeks, Jr.

A W. W. Norton Book
Published by
Grosset & Dunlap, Inc.
New York

HARDEMAN COUNTY LIBRARY
QUANAH, TEXAS

PHOTO CREDITS

Illustrative material courtesy of: Air France, xii, 95, 99, 177; Bahamas News Bureau, 7, 32, 35, 57, 60; British Overseas Airways Corp., 130, 150; British West Indies Airlines, 15, 144, 158, 167, 170; Columbus Memorial Library, 87; Curaçao Information Center, 135; French West Indies Tourist Board, 12, 41, 48, 155; Jamaica Tourist Board, 22, 27, 45, 82; Netherlands Antilles Government, 141; Netherlands West Indies Tourist Bureau, 138; Pan American Airways, 40; Pan American Union, 64, 69, 73, 79; Puerto Rico Economic Development Administration, 116, 117; Trinidad & Tobago Tourist Board, 185, 190; United Nations, 18, 178; United Press International, 106, 111, 197; U.S. Virgin Islands, 53.

Copyright © 1971 by Morris Weeks, Jr.
All Rights Reserved
Library of Congress Catalog Card Number: 78-153916
ISBN: 0-448-21408-3 (trade edition)
       0-448-26178-2 (library edition)
Published Simultaneously in Canada
Printed in the United States of America

CONTENTS

	Foreword	vii
1	Green Isles in the Sea	1
2	Living in Paradise (?)	10
3	Europe Plus Africa	19
4	How the Spaniards Came	28
5	Occupation: Pirate	37
6	Meet the Plantocrats	46
7	The Bahamas	54
8	Cuba	65
9	Jamaica	78
10	Haiti	89
11	The Dominican Republic	102
12	Puerto Rico	113
13	The Virgin Islands	123
14	The Netherlands Antilles	132
15	The English-Speaking Leewards	143
16	The French West Indies	153
17	The English-Speaking Windwards	163
18	Barbados	173
19	Trinidad and Tobago	181
20	Help!	193
	Recommended Reading	200
	Index	203

To Tony

FOREWORD

You never know what may happen when you set out to write a book.

This one took my wife and me to the West Indies three times in just over a year. Adding in earlier visits, we spent up to two weeks apiece on all the big islands and practically all the small ones. Our stay usually began and ended at an airport, but not always. We explored the Bahamas, the Grenadines, and part of the Virgin Islands by boat. We took the local cargo packet from St. Kitts to Nevis; then the skipper returned early, so we missed the boat and had to fly back (ten minutes) after all.

We were welcomed in Nevis and, among other islands, Jamaica, St. Maarten, Tobago, Martinique, Puerto Rico, and Bonaire. No one turned out even to say hello in Barbados, Guadeloupe, Curaçao, St. Thomas, or the Dominican Republic. We hit Trinidad when local unrest had caused a state of emergency to be imposed, with visitors barely tolerated. And in Haiti we almost were shot by a trigger-happy soldier because we were walking innocently along the sidewalk in front of the presidential palace. We had wondered why Haitians stayed off the sidewalk and walked in the street. The reason, we learned rather abruptly, was that Dictator François (Papa Doc) Duvalier wanted no one, Haitian or visitor, within hand-grenade range of his residence.

Does this suggest that the West Indies are numerous and varied? They are. Americans tend to lump them together as glamorous tropical hideaways notable mainly for palm trees, beaches, clear

FOREWORD

blue water, and, of course, sunshine. This is not unlike lumping all American cities together as prosaic workaday places notable mainly for streets, buildings, parks, and, of course, smog. You must get to know Minneapolis and New Orleans (or even Minneapolis and St. Paul) to see how different they are. The same is true of any two of the West Indies.

Our efforts in that direction required a lot of reading, looking, and talking. Several people made the job easier by arranging local accommodations, transportation, interviews, or all three. I want to thank particularly (from west to east) Fred Wilmot of the Jamaica Tourist Bureau; Josef Pons of the Puerto Rico Information Service; Julian Conner, Director of Tourism for St. Maarten; Henri Joseph, Director of Tourism on Martinique; John Van Ost of Caribbean Sailing Yachts, Inc., and Donald Bain, Director of the Trinidad and Tobago Tourist Bureau.

If this book helps Americans to a better understanding of the West Indies—and the West Indians—then it all has been worthwhile.

Morris Weeks, Jr.

HELLO, WEST INDIES

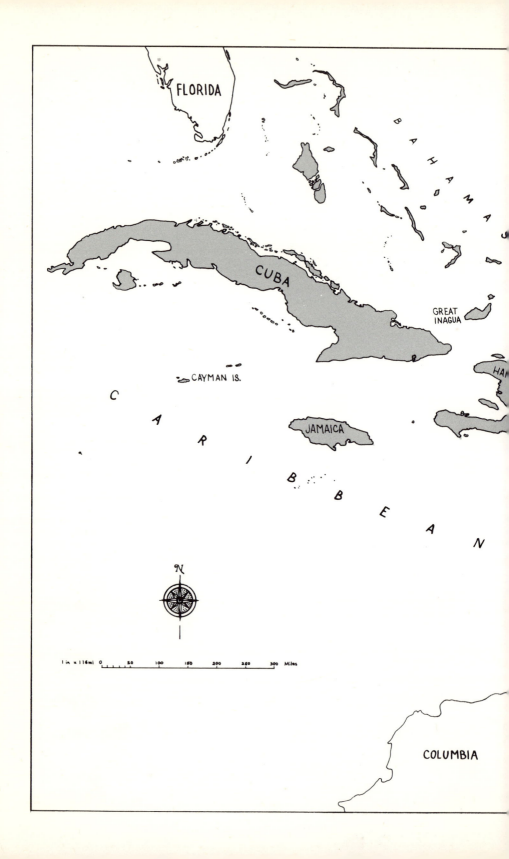

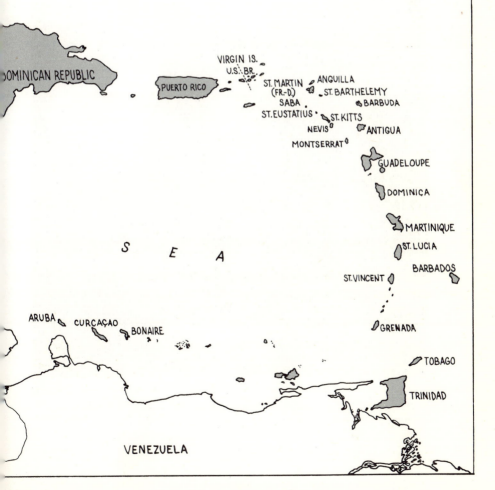

This is a typical landscape on a West Indian island that gets ample rain. Lofty tropical trees mantle the mountain slopes, while thick undergrowth crowds roads and land cleared for farming or grazing.

1

GREEN ISLES IN THE SEA

The year is 1493. The scene is a testimonial dinner for a notable citizen of Madrid, Spain. The tall, clean-shaven guest of honor chats with a companion. After the waiters have cleared the tables, the toastmaster stands up.

"Friends," he says, "tonight it's my privilege to introduce the man we're here to honor. He's an admiral, and a famous one. He took three little ships and proved that you *can* reach land by sailing west from Europe. Now he's going to tell you in his own words how he found a new route to India.

"Give him a hand, friends. Christopher Columbus!"

Columbus rises and smiles as the applause dies down. Then he starts his regular after-dinner speech. "Thank you, friends," he says, "but I'll have to correct that handsome introduction. You see, a funny thing happened to me on the way to India. I stubbed my toe on an island."

An appreciative chuckle goes up. . . .

This little joke never was made, of course. There were no testimonial dinners in 1493. Columbus wasn't known as a wit. And, though he eventually made four voyages to the New World, he died believing that he *had* found a route to India.

But there was no joke about that island. Columbus landed on it October 12, 1492 after a seemingly endless trip across an unknown ocean, and in gratitude named it San Salvador (Holy Savior). It proved to be just a sample. Apparently it was the small, flat island later renamed Watling (and still later re-renamed San Salvador), one of some 700 that make up the group now

2 HELLO, WEST INDIES

called the Bahamas. Columbus later discovered Cuba, Puerto Rico, Jamaica, and scores of smaller islands. He praised their tropical greenery, their golden beaches and crystalline water, their blazing sunshine and spice-scented shade, their friendly natives. But he called the natives Indians and the islands the West Indies. He never realized that *these* Indies were American, a huge, varied archipelago extending from Florida to Venezuela.

Others besides Columbus misnamed the islands. Many Europeans had heard the legend of idyllic Antillia, somewhere in the Western Ocean. Its people supposedly had evolved an ideal society in which everyone was happy. Columbus's first glowing reports made people think he had found Antillia. Mapmakers began using the name. Eventually it took the plural form Antilles.

Then there is the word Caribbean. (Americans usually stress this on the third syllable, Britons and former British colonials on the second.) Columbus found two Indian groups, Arawak and Carib, on various islands. The Arawaks were gentle and peaceable, and the aggressive Spaniards soon wiped them out. But the Caribs resisted for centuries (and a few are alive today). So Europeans called their islands the Caribees and their sea the Caribbean.

Columbus could not know how important the West Indies, or Antilles, or Caribees (take your pick) would become to the United States. That began later, after the English, French, and Dutch had colonized North America. By the mid-1600's the English settlers were trading with the West Indies. The islands also sent some prominent men to the mainland. One was peg-legged Pieter Stuyvesant, named governor of Dutch Nieuw Amsterdam after serving as governor of Curaçao (Kyoor-a-SO*) in the Caribbean. Another was Alexander Hamilton, born on Nevis (NE-vis) east of Puerto Rico, who became a founding father of the United States.

As our nation grew, it became possessive about the Caribbean. Colonies of friendly countries might be all right there, we said, but no unfriendly power would be allowed a foothold. In 1898 we found Spain unfriendly and shoved her out of Cuba and Puerto Rico. Later we sent troops to Haiti and the Dominican

* Pronunciations given in this book are approximate.

GREEN ISLES IN THE SEA 3

Republic to keep things peaceful. During World War II we established bases on several islands to protect the Panama Canal. In 1962 we forced the withdrawal of Soviet missiles from Cuba. In 1970, when Russia was reported building a nuclear-submarine base in Cuba, our government naturally showed great concern.

American industry has found the West Indies a source of raw materials—chiefly sugar, coffee, bananas, cocoa, spices, and other agricultural products—and a market for manufactured goods of many kinds, from chewing gum to prefabricated houses. In recent years, however, most other trade has been overshadowed by tourism. Americans in growing numbers (along with Canadians, Britons, and other Europeans) share Columbus's view of the islands.

The map on pages x-xi lays them out for inspection—the main ones, anyway, since there is no room for thousands of islets, cays (pronounced keys), and charted rocks that are part of the total.

The West Indies lie in an arc from northwest to southeast, almost touching the mainland at both ends. They occupy an area about 1,700 miles long and 1,200 miles wide—nearly the size of the United States east of Colorado. They cut off from the Atlantic Ocean both the Caribbean Sea (970,000 square miles) and the Gulf of Mexico (580,000). The islands themselves cover less than 100,000 square miles, and nearly half of that is Cuba (almost as big as Pennsylvania). Some well-known islands are practically bumps in the water. All of the United States Virgin Islands, beloved of tourists, would fit neatly into the city of Philadelphia.

The Antilles comprise three main groups from north to south.

First come the Bahamas, an archipelago in themselves, some 4,500 square miles of flat, almost treeless land strewn across 100,000 square miles of water. If the northermost Bahama cay were over Chicago, the others would trail southeast to Norfolk, Virginia. The Commonwealth of the Bahamas was a British colony until 1964.

Southward, in a rough west-to-east line, lie the four big islands called the Greater Antilles: Cuba, Jamaica, Hispaniola, and Puerto Rico. All are mountainous—Hispaniola's Pico Duarte (PE-co DWAHR-tay), at 10,206 feet, is the highest in the Carib-

4   HELLO, WEST INDIES

bean—as well as fertile and densely populated. These were the islands most important to the Spaniards. On them are three countries of strongly Spanish background: Cuba, the Dominican Republic (which shares Hispaniola with formerly French Haiti), and Puerto Rico.

All the remaining islands fall into the Lesser Antilles. There are two groups. One stretches like an emerald necklace from the Virgin Islands, very close to Puerto Rico, 600 miles southeast to Trinidad, off eastern Venezuela. These islands are so close that one usually can be seen from the next. The other group is scattered along the South American coast toward Central America. Most of the Lesser Antilles were European possessions until recently, or still are.

Considering their size, the islands show striking differences. Take language. Spain's early claims to the whole area were vigorously contested by other powers, and today Spanish may be spoken on one island, French on another, English on a third, with Dutch, Danish, or local patois in between. On some Dutch islands everyone speaks English. On some English islands most people speak French. On Trinidad, where English is official, some people speak Arabic.

Or take government. After centuries of remote control from distant capitals, most islanders now have more or less self-rule. The English islands (with minor exceptions) have become virtually independent since World War II. The French islands have been made integral units of France, just as Hawaii has become a state. The Dutch islands have become equal partners with the Netherlands. Haiti and the Dominican Republic became independent in the early 1800's, but still are trying to establish stable governments. The same was true of Cuba (independent since 1898) until Fidel Castro turned it into a communist dictatorship. Puerto Rico enjoys unique status as a commonwealth associated with the United States.

There are many other differences between islands. Yet most of them have much in common:
● All share a stable climate, averaging from about 70 to 85 degrees the year round. Heat and humidity prevail at sea level, but temperatures drop with altitude. Even a thousand feet up, the air

GREEN ISLES IN THE SEA   5

usually is cool and fresh. Most of the area has two main seasons, wet (roughly May through November) and dry.

• Up to 95 percent of the people on most islands are black or mulatto. Their ancestors were slaves, brought from Africa to work haciendas or plantations established by Europeans. The percentage of blacks is lowest on the formerly Spanish islands.

• Practically every island is overpopulated and getting more so. Total population has risen *400 percent* since 1900, from a bit over six million to about 24 million. The Antillean birthrate is among the highest on earth. So is the rate of illegitimate births.

• Few islands have any natural resources beyond sunshine, rain, and limited fertile soil. Most depend heavily on one or two export crops, such as sugar or bananas. The main exceptions are Cuba, with valuable deposits of nickel, copper, and manganese; Jamaica, the world's top exporter of bauxite (the ore from which aluminum is extracted); and Trinidad, an important source of petroleum and asphalt.

• Unemployment is a serious problem throughout the area. Growing tropical crops no longer utilizes the manpower of slave days. Some islanders have found work by emigrating to North America or Europe, and more would like to. Many believe that industrialization—the building of factories to create jobs—can cure all ills. Only Puerto Rico, Curaçao, and Trinidad have made real progress in that direction. For the rest, factories are a poor prospect and (except in Cuba) tourism is the best hope.

• While the island governments grapple with their problems, solutions come hard—and criticism mounts. Some islanders say their leaders care more for the approval of foreigners and whites than for the good of their own people. On some islands this feeling leads to cries for leftist "solutions" such as Castro brought Cuba. On some former British islands, where blacks are a huge majority but mulattoes run the government, there are demands for "Black Power"—meaning an end to the favored treatment the mulatto leaders allegedly give white landowners and businessmen.

Most of the islands are closely connected, under water. Millions of years ago a mountain range ran from Central America to Venezuela. Natural forces gradually lowered it until only the

6   HELLO, WEST INDIES

higher peaks and valleys were exposed. (The Bahamas and a few other "fringe" islands are essentially coral reefs, as is Bermuda, in the Atlantic some 580 miles off North Carolina.) The nearby sea floor was squeezed into trenches sometimes deeper than the ocean itself. Not far north of Hispaniola the bottom has been measured at 28,374 feet, nearly five and a half miles straight down.

The subterranean pressures left the islands somewhat unstable, with volcanoes and recurrent earthquakes. Some small islands are little more than volcanic cones. On others there are craters filled with steam and the reek of sulfur from activity just underground. The standard word for such a crater is the French *soufrière* (soo-fre-AIR). One volcano proved that all still may become violent. It is Mont Pelée, on Martinique, which in 1902 erupted and killed 30,000 persons.

So much for the islands' underpinnings. We are concerned more with what shows above water—which may not be much. The islands offer only slight obstacles to the movement of air and ocean currents, and are deeply involved with both.

Thus, apart from the persistent sunshine, the weather feature of the West Indies is the trade wind. This actually is a global air movement. It traverses the Atlantic in a largely southwesterly direction the year round, blowing almost constantly across the Antilles. The early explorers, not to mention later Spanish treasure fleets and the pirates who preyed on them, trusted the trade wind to push their sail-powered vessels. Today it serves island fishermen, makes yachtsmen happy, and tempers the hot sun for everyone.

Because of the wind, the chief port (usually the capital) of almost every island is on the sheltered lee side. The main exceptions are La Habana, Cuba, and San Juan, Puerto Rico—each on the exposed north coast, but with a good-sized, protected harbor.

Europeans grouped the Lesser Antilles largely by their position relative to the wind. The Spaniards logically gave the name Windward to the northeastern islands directly in the wind's path—the group from the Virgin Islands "around the bend" to Guadeloupe —while those to the south, being less exposed, were called Lee-

Flat land and shallow water mark a coral island in the Antilles. Here it is easy to lay out towns and build houses. But water for domestic use may have to come from wells, or from desalting sea water.

8   HELLO, WEST INDIES

ward. Later, when the English came to govern most of the same islands, they illogically reversed things. Their Leewards ran around the bend and their Windwards were south—to leeward.

The British usage still prevails for those islands. But the Dutch, who own six Antilles, apply Spanish logic: those to the northeast, surrounded by British Leewards, are Dutch Windwards, while their Leewards lie well off to the southwest. The French ignore the whole business and call their islands by name only.

In any case, the trade wind keeps the Caribbean watered. Crossing the ocean, it picks up moisture that later drops as rain —though often not until the wind hits high ground. Flat little Antigua, in the northeastern corner, averages about 40 inches of rain a year, while the peaks of Dominica, 90 miles south, are inundated by 360 inches.* The southeastern islands generally are green while southwestern ones are dry and brown. On the Greater Antilles, where the mountains trend east and west, the trade wind waters the north coasts while the south suffer frequent droughts.

Besides all this, the wind strongly affects the sea. In its passage across 3,000 miles of ocean it builds up long rollers. These dash against the islands' eastern shores or, funneling between them (average speed: 11 to 20 miles a day), surge on through the Caribbean. When the water finally reaches the mainland, it piles up and must escape northward. Some of it crowds into the Gulf of Mexico. The rest veers northeast and rushes back into the Atlantic in a narrow torrent between Cuba and Florida—the Gulf Stream.

Finally, the trade wind is involved in a major feature of West Indian weather that sometimes breaks out and ravages the mainland. This is the dreaded hurricane. (The word comes from the Carib *huracán*. Europeans never had heard of hurricanes before Columbus.) The typical hurricane is born between June and November, somewhere in the Atlantic. The air becomes disturbed, rises, and starts to circle. Following the trade-wind track, it picks up speed and grows bigger. It may curve northward and die out over the ocean. Or it may plunge ahead to lash the Antilles.

The islands have little defense. Wind of more than 75 miles an

---

* These two islands are pronounced An-TEE-ga and Doe-min-E-ca, respectively. Other unexpected pronunciations in the Lesser Antilles include St. Lucia (LOO-sha), Grenada (Gre-NAY-da), and Barbados (Bar-BAY-doce).

GREEN ISLES IN THE SEA 9

hour (official hurricane speed) can flatten a sugarcane plantation, rip up acres of productive trees, take roofs off well-built
homes and demolish shacks. It can sink ships or pile them up on
shore. It can dump incredible volumes of rain. (In Cuba, a 1967
hurricane brought 78 inches in five days.) One such assault may
kill hundreds of persons and erase an island's livelihood. The survivors shrug, set about rebuilding, and wait long years for prosperity to return.

Yet between killer winds the islands have sunshine and sudden
short showers, warmth and peace and beauty. Five days after
sighting San Salvador, Columbus wrote: "This land is the best
and most fertile and temperate and flat and good that can be
found in the world." He was wrong about India, but many people
would say he was right about the Indies.

2

LIVING IN PARADISE (?)

If the preceding chapter talks a lot about the climate of the West Indies, it is because climate is the number one factor in the way West Indians live.

Overall, the Antillean climate is kindly toward man. It makes the essentials of life much easier to come by than in most of the United States. Buildings require no heat. (Rather, they usually need all the ventilation they can get.) Just about everyone wears light, inexpensive clothing the year round, and millions of people go barefoot. Roads never are blocked by snow, antifreeze is unknown, and the only skiing is the kind you do on water.

More important, the climate makes things grow. Tropical fruits—coconuts, mangoes, bananas, breadfruit, papayas, and many others—hang heavy on the trees. Vegetables are easy to raise, especially the starchy root crop called cassava or manioc (which long filled much the same dietary need in the Antilles as corn and potatoes elsewhere). Add the great variety of fish in the sea, and no one is likely to starve.

The Indians in their day got along without working too hard, and so do many modern islanders. If a man has a plot of land big enough to grow food for his family, keep a few chickens, and raise a little to sell, he doesn't need much else. After work he can rest in the shade, drowse in the sun, take a swim, go fishing, play with his children. . . . Sounds like paradise, doesn't it?

In some ways it does indeed. But the climate has other, less favorable effects on life in the West Indies.

For one, conditions in the tropics may be *too* easy. They can

LIVING IN PARADISE (?)   11

cut down energy and ambition. Continuous hot weather may make for a great vacation, but as a steady diet it can be monotonous. People usually are most energetic and productive where the climate is cooler and varies every few days or so.

Heat and humidity also encourage disease. In the West Indies, malaria and yellow fever killed natives and immigrants alike until doctors found that both are caused by organisms transmitted by the bite of certain warm-climate mosquitoes. Once the mosquitoes were controlled, the diseases were too. But they could return quickly if the controls were relaxed.

The most serious criticism of the West Indian climate, however, is that it led to Negro slavery throughout the islands. No one planned it that way—but it happened.

The first Spanish conquistadors were looking for gold. When the islands yielded practically none, the Spaniards turned to another source of wealth: tropical crops. The islands were ideal for the establishment of big haciendas (plantations or estates) planted with sugar, spices, indigo, cotton, or other things that in those days brought high prices in Europe.

Indians were expected to work the haciendas, but the Indians all too soon were killed off. Rather than give up their "green gold," the Spaniards began importing slaves from Africa. The first shipload arrived even before Columbus's fourth voyage. That set the pattern for three centuries of forced labor on every island that Europeans colonized.

Slavery was monstrous, cruel, inhuman. It brutalized both the slaves and their masters. It also turned out to be poor business. The unpaid labor of millions of blacks made possible huge harvests and huge returns for the white landowners. But when the Industrial Revolution began to transform Europe, the West Indies were encouraged to keep producing raw materials. Eventually their markets became glutted. As profits fell off, a sad discovery emerged: dependence on free labor had kept the Caribbean from sharing in the industrial surge of the Western world. The islands still are trying to catch up.

Slavery finally ended on all the islands during the nineteenth century, but many of its aftereffects linger on. One of the worst results from the almost complete breakdown of the family unit

Haggling over the price of small items is relished by West Indian venders and housewives alike. Among the goods visible in this market are tomatoes, root vegetables, eggs, beans, and brooms.

among the slaves. Husbands, wives, and children often were separated even before they left Africa. Later, every family was at the mercy of a white owner. A slave who fathered children could not provide for them and had no control over their lives. In such circumstances, most black men stopped even trying to take responsibility for their children. Families were held together, if at all, by women. Temporary unions became commonplace and the great majority of children were illegitimate.

This pattern became so deeply ingrained that it still prevails in many parts of the West Indies. It raises a probing question for the future: Can a nation be stable unless the families that make it up are stable?

LIVING IN PARADISE (?)   13

Similarly, the white owners denied practically all slaves an education beyond that needed for plantation jobs. When freedom came, few blacks were equipped to take advantage of it. Farm work was what they knew, so most of them stayed on the land. Many became small farmers (and many of their descendants still are). Some found paid work on the big estates that managed to keep going (and some of their descendants still do). A few moved to town and more skilled jobs. Their chance to rise remained slim, for whites stood in the way.

Today the picture is changing, but finding work remains a problem. The average plot of land yields just so much. It cannot supply a protein-rich diet. (Protein malnutrition is common in the Caribbean.) It does not produce clothes, pay the taxes, or provide even such modest conveniences as ironing boards or kerosene stoves. For such things a man needs a job that will bring in cash.

If he lives in town, he has more choices than in the past. He may clerk in a store or office, open a small business, drive a bus or taxi, sell souvenirs to tourists, do odd jobs. He may find work on the waterfront or in commercial fishing. There are a good many government jobs, from road construction to the post office. If his island has some industry, such as an oil refinery or a bauxite mine, he may be taken on, join a union, and achieve some security.

If he is a rural dweller, his best bet for paid work probably is the nearest estate that grows a crop requiring a lot of hand labor to plant, cultivate, or harvest. Most such jobs are seasonal. Sugarcane, for example, cannot give employment more than eight months a year at best. The man who needs a job the rest of the time may not find it. The search for work leads many West Indians not only from country to town but from island to island, or beyond. (Close to 100,000 persons live on Grenada, for example, but nearly that many have emigrated to the United States.) Unemployment and poverty are two continuing mementoes of the slave centuries.

Island housing also tends to reflect colonial days. At the height of the "plantocracy" (the white landowner class), each estate was almost a feudal domain. Its heart was the great house, de-

14 HELLO, WEST INDIES

signed and furnished with small regard for expense. By contrast, the slaves who made it possible were sheltered in huts that barely kept out the weather. Such quarters were cheap and easy to build, and still are. You see them dotted along country roads or packed into urban blocks—one- or two-room shacks, made of any available materials (poles and palm thatch, boards and corrugated iron) and furnished with only the bare necessities.

Income levels have been rising, of course, and with them the caliber of housing. Many island homes retain a simple floor plan but are sturdily constructed of concrete block, stone, or brick. Often they are painted in bright colors and boast a porch, a yard splashed with tropical flowers, a strip of lawn, a carport— and, if the family can swing it, a TV antenna. On some islands the government is moving low-income families into modern apartments or housing developments, though rarely fast enough to meet the demand.

Some of the great houses have fallen into ruins. Others shelter descendants of the old plantocracy. Others have been sold (usually to Americans, Canadians, or Britons) for use as vacation homes or tourist resorts.

One of the most marked changes since colonial times is the growth of towns and cities. Originally they served as the local seats of European government and gradually acquired such residents as merchants, shipbuilders, doctors, their families—and their slaves. The average town looked much like a town in the "home country." Some still do.

The main town on a small island (or a small one on a larger island) often consists of a few blocks of one- and two-story buildings, generally of wood or stone, sometimes painted in pastel shades and often iron roofed. Streets are narrow: they were laid out for foot or horse-drawn traffic, not the motor vehicles that now create small but knotty traffic jams. (When they do, few drivers get upset. A blocked street, they indicate, is just part of

The sea furnishes a living for thousands of islanders, while its fish help to feed millions more. These fishermen are attending to an essential chore: mending their nets before putting them to work.

16   HELLO, WEST INDIES

their unhurried island life.) Many buildings, built decades ago, have weathered badly in the beating sun. Newer structures in today's international concrete-steel-glass style are mostly schools, hospitals, or other public buildings.

Larger cities look rather like those in the southern United States or tropical Latin America. The four biggest—La Habana, San Juan, Santo Domingo (Dominican Republic), and Kingston (Jamaica)—have more than a half million residents each. They have many white and light-colored buildings, streets often lined with trees (particularly palms), lots of flowers, and blue water generally a few blocks away. Traffic may be really thick, especially at rush hours. It often is complicated by swarms of motor-cycles and bicycles, and by slow-moving carts and wagons. Most cities have fewer traffic lights and more traffic policemen than American cities of like size. The policemen tend to be soft voiced, polite, and efficient. On former British islands they often cut a dashing figure in well-pressed shorts and short-sleeved shirts above clean dark shoes and knee-length socks, all topped off with a white Sam Browne belt and a white pith helmet.

Even in the biggest cities, the countryside never seems far away. Except for high-rise office buildings and hotels—largely in La Habana and San Juan—hardly a structure in the Antilles tops five stories. Air-conditioned buses may ply main avenues, but on side streets a pig or a goat may be wandering, or a cow pastured in a vacant lot.

West Indian cities, like cities everywhere, lately have grown at a record clip. The short distances on most islands make it easy to pack up and move to town, and a great many people have done just that. Working the land no longer appeals to them. They say it is "beneath them." This may come originally from associating farm labor with slavery, but probably most people are drawn by city life—the activity and variety, the stores and amusements, the contacts with other people.

In some areas, as a result, there no longer are enough workers to harvest all the crops as they ripen. Some Puerto Rican sugar growers recruit cane cutters from the Dominican Republic (where wages are lower), while some Dominican growers re-cruit from Haiti (where wages are lower still). On St. Croix in

LIVING IN PARADISE (?)   17

the U.S. Virgin Islands, a sugar island for centuries, cane now grows wild for lack of cutters. Fidel Castro's troubles in securing "volunteers" to harvest Cuban cane have been widely reported.

At the same time, island cities have not been able to absorb all their new residents comfortably. In San Juan, in Kingston, and in Port of Spain, Trinidad, to take some of the worst examples, rural immigrants have helped create extensive slums. These are distinguished by the poorest kind of housing, a scarcity of such basic needs as electricity, water, and toilets, and a high rate of joblessness, school dropouts, juvenile delinquency, drug addiction, illegitimate births, and crime. None of that sounds like "living in paradise," but it is a fact of West Indian life today.

Interlocked with the need for more jobs is the need for better education to handle them. Recent years have seen a steady upward movement of blacks into positions once labeled "White Only" in government, business, and the professions, but the average islander still gets far too little schooling. In slave days, blacks rarely were taught even to read and write. Emancipation brought primary schools, but never enough of them. Today free public education in primary school (grades 1–6) is generally available on every island, in secondary school (grades 7–9) on most, and through grade 12 on some. Church and private schools try to take up the slack where they can.

Higher education is limited to a few advanced institutes, colleges, and universities. Two of the last, both founded centuries ago, still function in Cuba and the Dominican Republic. The University of Puerto Rico, born as a teachers' college soon after the United States acquired the island, has become the biggest in the Antilles. The University of the West Indies was established in 1948 with headquarters on Jamaica. It has campuses there, on Trinidad, and on Barbados, and is supported by 14 English-speaking islands in proportion to their population.

Schooling on most islands still tends to be modeled on teaching methods and textbooks brought from the "home country," but island educators gradually are adapting those to local needs. It takes time—and money. Most island governments are spending just about all they can on education, but the amounts vary with local conditions. So do the results. Barbados, a trimly British

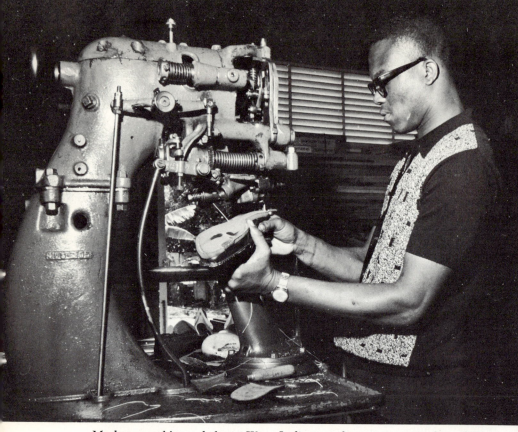

Modern machinery helps a West Indian workman turn out shoes better and faster than he ever could have done by hand. Every island has hopes of more such industry, but only a few have had luck to date.

island with a long, peaceful history, boasts the very high figure of 97 percent literacy. In poverty-stricken Haiti, cursed by civil strife ever since the slaves threw out their French rulers, the figure may not top 20 percent.

College graduates remain a tiny minority on every island. Those with specialized training often find greater rewards abroad than at home, so there is a small but steady "brain drain" from the Antilles to North America and Europe. Yet many do stay home because they see a need and want to help answer it.

From such educated persons, of whatever color, the islands' leaders are being drawn. They have at least one advantage over the leaders of most other lands. This is the pace of island life and the constant presence of sunshine, sand, and sea. When problems pile up, escape is close at hand. Even a prime minister can find time to rest in the shade, take a swim, go fishing, play with his children. . . . It could be worse.

3

EUROPE PLUS AFRICA

On the former British island of St. Vincent, near the southeastern end of the Lesser Antilles, a fourteen-year-old boy hefts a flat bat and steps up for the next pitch. He swings and connects. His teammates shout as he scores the 34th run of the game—which is cricket.

On the former Spanish island of Puerto Rico, well up in the Greater Antilles, a fourteen-year-old boy hefts a round bat and steps up for the next pitch. He swings and connects. His teammates shout as he scores the only run of the game—which is baseball.

Such similar moments in otherwise different sports highlight probably the most important factor, after climate, in the way West Indians live. This is that daily life on every island has been patterned on—and modified by—the customs, interests, and viewpoints of the people who settled that island. To put it as a question: Where did all the islanders come from?

One answer is Europe. The West Indies were settled by much the same sorts of Europeans who settled North America (pushing aside or wiping out the Amerindians in each case), and at much the same time. The islands, however, stayed under colonial rule far longer than the mainland. Today the differences from island to island often are greater than those from, say, French Canada to Ohio to Guatemala. The most obvious difference is in language, but there are others that run through the whole fabric of people's lives.

Take something as unremarkable as food. In the raw state, it

20 HELLO, WEST INDIES

is much the same throughout the Antilles. Native cooks prepare the basic dishes—soups, fried fish, meat stews, boiled vegetables —in much the same way everywhere. But if you visit Antigua and then Guadeloupe, about 60 miles away, you should be happily surprised at the improvement in the meals. Guadeloupe was colonized by Frenchmen and shows the French flair with such things as sauces, cheese, salads, and wine, while Antiguan cooking originated in the uninspired kitchens of England. Food on Cuba and Puerto Rico reflects the Spanish taste for beans, rice, and garlic. On Trinidad, Hindu cooking is widely popular. On some Dutch islands the specialty is *rijsttafel* (RACE-ta-fel), a huge, many-course meal from the East Indies.

Beverage preferences also vary. The English brought with them a devotion to tea, which still is essential at mealtimes and during office "tea breaks" on all the English-speaking islands. Elsewhere, coffee is king. The two drinks universally enjoyed are rum (of which almost every island produces its own brand) and American-style bottled colas and other soft drinks.

So with many other things. Consider such a trivial matter as the direction of auto traffic. The English drive on the left, so people on the former British islands do too. Everyone else drives on the right, with one baffling exception: the U.S. Virgin Islands.

The British passion for cricket made that a major sport on Jamaica, Barbados, Trinidad, and a number of smaller islands. There it stops. The Spanish, French, and Dutch were partial to soccer football, so that generally became the top sport on their islands. The Americans introduced baseball to Puerto Rico and the Virgin Islands. It soon caught on also in neighboring Cuba and the Dominican Republic—though not in Haiti, which lies directly between them.

Track and field is popular on all islands (and usually called "athletics"), in part because running and jumping did not originate in just one colonial nation. Basketball also is popular; though an American invention, it is played just about everywhere on earth. Athletics and basketball are almost the only sports that draw entries from every country in the Central American and Caribbean Games (a regional edition of the worldwide Olympic Games).

EUROPE PLUS AFRICA   21

So the white colonists brought basic cultural elements to all the islands, from language to clothing and education to religion. Most islanders still live in the patterns thus established. But there is another element. No matter how many people came originally from Europe, in most of the Caribbean they soon were outnumbered by Africans and eventually almost submerged by them.

The slaves were brought from many areas of west Africa, representing many different tribes, customs, and beliefs. Their white masters tried to insure that black family ties were broken, native languages forgotten, tribal identities destroyed. But the slaves managed—by sheer numbers as much as anything else—to hold onto some of their old ways and beliefs. Though many learned to speak and dress and even think like Europeans, the "Europeanization" rarely was complete. Often it was little more than skin deep.

The slaves fresh from Africa often could not talk to one another until they learned at least a few words of their masters' language. That in turn became the basis of a new dialect, simplified and ungrammatical, usually with a few words from other languages as well. The dialect was handed down from one slave generation to the next, thus preserving some words long after the whites stopped using them. As new slaves arrived, they learned the dialect but added African words to it. Most slaves thus acquired two increasingly different languages, their masters' and their own. After slavery ended, the languages continued side by side. This explains why today the visitor to any island may be baffled when two natives speak to each other, though he normally understands what they say to *him*.

Besides setting up new cultural patterns and partially preserving old ones, the slaves passed along Negro qualities to their children and, to a lesser degree, to the mulattoes of mixed blood. With emancipation, blacks and mulattoes alike were able to take a larger part in island life. The recent trend toward independence has given those of African descent new opportunities and influence.

Thus the average islander's life is cast in a European mold, but with many non-European aspects. These tend to cut across every island regardless of its colonial past.

One of England's gifts to the Caribbean is cricket. Here white-clad native players show their skill. The bowler has hurled the ball at the wicket, and the batter waits tensely to try to hit it, then run.

Consider West Indian music. For centuries the white settlers listened to, and sometimes performed, the works of European composers. They sang hymns and popular ballads. They enjoyed such relatively restrained dances as the minuet, mazurka, waltz, and *pasodoble* (pa-so-DOE-blay). Bit by bit they also became familiar with the music, and particularly the dancing, of their slaves.

Dancing had a special meaning for the blacks. In the hot climate of Africa, where most daily events transpired outdoors, they had developed a variety of dances for all kinds of occasions,

EUROPE PLUS AFRICA 23

from celebration of the harvest to worship of their gods. The West Indian climate encouraged the same kind of activity. And dancing often was the slaves' only escape from the harsh realities of their life. On a tropical night, in a clearing lit by torches, with drums thudding and no white boss giving orders, a slave might even dream for a few hours that he was free.

The importance of dancing was noted early. Jean Labat (La-BA), an observant French priest who visited Martinique in the late 1600's, described a dance called the calenda that apparently came from Africa's Guinea coast. It began rather formally, with men and women in separate lines that approached each other, then retreated. A beat was supplied by drums made from hollow tree trunks. Gradually the beat speeded up, and so did the dancing. Couples formed, broke away, and reformed. Finally the dance reached a violent climax.

Some slaveowners banned the calenda as improper. But it spread through the Antilles and became so popular that even nuns danced it. It combined compelling rhythm with challenging footwork, and released pent-up feelings. These were hallmarks of African dancing, not European.

Some two centuries later, the American composer-pianist Louis Gottschalk spent several years in the Antilles and was deeply impressed. "The dance of the Negroes," he wrote, "involves a whole poetry; quiverings, serpentine undulations, repressed passion. . . ." By contrast, European-American dancing was "sickly gymnastics performed in the company of a pretty woman." Gottschalk was the first musician of international stature to note and admire Afro-Antillean rhythm and melody, and he made use of both in many of his own works.

The elements identified by Labat and Gottschalk appear in such modern West Indian dances as the rumba, conga, mambo, beguine, merengue, and cha-cha. The sound of all of them is familiar to most Americans. We recognize the use of drums, maracas, scrapers, and other typical rhythm instruments, and the intricate way that melody and beat are interwoven. Often we call the result Latin American, since these dances come from Spanish- or French-speaking islands. But their birthplace is Africa.

Folklore also has helped preserve some of Africa in the West

24 HELLO, WEST INDIES

Indies. This includes the old stories and songs, not to mention the superstitions, whose authors have been forgotten but which are handed down from parent to child. Every culture has them. Europeans brought theirs to the islands, and some survive intact, as in certain songs sung to children's games. But most were modified by the impact of slave speech and background. A lover's lament for his blonde darling might become the sad story of how the singer lost his dark-skinned, dark-haired beauty. French dragons might become Haitian alligators. Or an African folk tale might be passed along almost unchanged. In this category are the Anancy stories still popular on Jamaica, Trinidad, and some other islands. Anancy, the central character of them all, is a clever spider who triumphs over all kinds of situations by fast thinking.

The West Indies have produced their share of popular songs. Originally European in form—such as the well-known *La Paloma,* composed in Cuba in the mid-1800's but essentially Spanish—they have taken on a Caribbean quality all their own. Not all reach the United States. For example, many are written each year for Carnival, the period of merrymaking on almost every island just before the start of Lent. Some Carnival songs win prizes and make their composers small fortunes. The rest soon are forgotten.

There also is formal music and dance, utilizing such advanced techniques as composition, orchestration, and choreography. The Antilles have produced little formal music, but a number of dance companies exist—again reflecting the African element—and some of their offerings have won high critical praise. Among individual dancers at least two have won fame outside the islands: Geoffrey Holder of Trinidad and Alicia Alonso of Cuba.

But this is getting away from daily life. Overall, probably the most striking aspects of the merger of Europe and Africa is in the field of religion.

The Spaniards planted the Catholic Church wherever they settled. So did the French. The British brought the Anglican faith (represented today in the United States by the Episcopal Church). The Dutch brought a tradition of religious freedom, today the rule on all the islands. But the various Christian churches have had a powerful influence.

EUROPE PLUS AFRICA   25

Each faith began by giving its white members spiritual guidance and advice on manners and morals. Under slavery, priests and ministers undertook to do the same for the blacks. Many slaves found comfort in this. Torn from their own tribal gods, thrust into a strange world of toil and chains, they welcomed the concept of a heavenly father who would love them (they were promised) if they would only believe in him. For generations they did so, or professed to. Most blacks to this day vow allegiance to one or another Christian faith, and on Sunday mornings most islands blossom out like flower gardens with the clean, starched or ruffled dresses and hats, colored in every hue, of women and girls on their way to and from church.

Yet Christianity rarely was fully understood or accepted by the slaves. Its sole deity not only was invisible and untouchable but also forbade the making of idols, whereas most African religions abounded in nature gods, present in everything from rocks to stars, and symbolized in sculptures, masks, and the like. It did not seem right to let go of the old gods entirely. So a kind of underground religion grew up, generally based on nature worship but often adding figures from Christian teaching—saints, angels, prophets, apostles, and so on.

The end product may be seen on most islands today. It plays a widely varying part in people's lives. Many islanders are good Christians, and some take the Bible so literally that their arguments over its meaning have led to the formation of small "splinter" churches, each following what it regards as the revealed truth. Other islanders are equally good Hindus, Moslems, Buddhists, or Jews. Some have no religion. But millions still revere, to some degree, the old gods of tribal Africa.

In some cases their belief does not run much above the level of superstition. People may sleep with their windows closed to keep out night-roaming evil spirits. Or they may buy amulets and colored candles to help along their prayers for success in a new job, or in love. But there also are full-fledged pagan religions with recognized meeting places, an organized system of priests and helpers, regular forms of observance, and sometimes spectacular activities.

The outstanding example is voodoo, best known in Haiti. It is

26 HELLO, WEST INDIES

based on belief in spirits that may aid troubled mortals if approached the right way. The approach is through a long ceremony, involving drums, dancing, animal sacrifice, and other African elements. People may stay up all night at a voodoo ceremony, then go directly to morning mass with an untroubled conscience.

Somewhat similar faiths may be found elsewhere—*pukkumina* on Jamaica, *shango* on Grenada, spiritism on Cuba and Puerto Rico. Even enlightened islanders may believe in ghosts, or in the power of *obeah* (black magic) to cause harm. Many island governments have outlawed obeah, but it still is practiced to some extent almost everywhere. These things exist side by side with conventional religion and even supply formal cultural elements, as when the Jamaica National Dance Theater choreographs and stages a *pukkumina* ritual.

In sum, Europe and Africa have joined to create a new way of life in the West Indies. And, like the islanders themselves, it still is evolving.

At a pukkumina *ceremony in Jamaica, the "shepherd" exhorts his "flock" with Afro-European fervor. The woman beside him holds maracas to supply rhythm for dancing when the "flock" responds.*

4

HOW THE SPANIARDS CAME

Once upon a time there *was* a paradise in the West Indies. It was inhabited solely by animals and Indians.

Picture the kind of tropical island we have been talking about. Take away the towns and plantations, the airports and hotels. From beach to mountain top the land is green, warm, quiet, and seemingly empty. The trees bear abundant fruit and there are edible roots and berries. Insects feed on these things, along with birds of many colors. Small mammals thrive—armadillos, muskrats, raccoons, monkeys, various rodents—but no predators or poisonous snakes. All these creatures reached the islands, step by slow step, from the American mainland.

So did the Indians. Members of the Arawak language family, they are believed to have come from the Orinoco or Amazon basins of South America. Many stayed on the mainland, but some moved northward by dugout canoe (we get this word from the Arawak *canoa*) until they were spread throughout the Lesser Antilles. Generally they stopped in one place for some time, living in a way that people today can only dream about.

Records of the Arawaks are few, but we know they could exist comfortably with minimum effort. Food was for the taking. Life posed few challenges. Day followed day in a slow procession, from sunrise through morning heat to the high glare of noon, then gradual cooling (perhaps helped by showers), a flaming sunset, and star-drenched night. Through it all the trade wind blew like a caress.

Each Arawak tribe was basically a group sharing the same ter-

HOW THE SPANIARDS CAME 29

ritory and food resources. The leader was the *cacique* (ca-SE-kay). There were priests, for the Arawaks believed in a supreme being and in lesser gods called *zemis* (*SAY*-mees). These were represented by crude idols of stone, wood, and other substances, including gold.

Arawak houses were very simple, wood frames thatched with palm leaves. They wore little or no clothing, though a species of cotton is native to the West Indies and from it they made hammocks. (We get this word from the Arawak *hamac*.) They grew corn and yams, made shell utensils and ornaments, and turned out some good brown pottery. But they never worked too hard at anything. They preferred to swim, play ball, or unlimber their drums and dance. Their only known artistic effort was to scratch or paint truly primitive figures (most of them look like the work of kindergarteners) on rocks and inside caves.

The Arawaks had weapons—wooden clubs, and on some islands bows and arrows—but they rarely raised them in anger. When one tribe fought another, it usually was more a contest than a battle.

For several centuries the Arawaks migrated slowly north and west, eventually reaching Puerto Rico. There and beyond they found a simple hunting people, the Siboney (Se-bo-NAY), of whom we know practically nothing. The Arawaks evidently took over the Greater Antilles in a slow, relaxed sort of way. By the late fifteenth century the area supported an estimated three million Indians in warm, happy idleness.

Only one thing disturbed their eden: the fierce, warlike Caribs, who had followed the Arawaks all the way from South America. The Caribs were something rare indeed: human beings who killed others specifically to eat them. Other cannibals have eaten human flesh for religious reasons, or because they were starving, but the Caribs did so by choice. Usually they devoured the males of any tribe they defeated in battle, and enslaved the women. (The name Carib, slightly changed in the hearing, became our word cannibal.) The Arawaks were no match for these dedicated warriors. When Carib raiders appeared on an Arawak island, the occupants knew more would follow and did their best to escape.

The Caribs reached the small islands east of Puerto Rico about

30 HELLO, WEST INDIES

the time the Arawaks were well distributed to the west. Carib raids on Puerto Rico, in fact, had already begun. Then came the day that changed everything forever for Arawak and Carib alike.

That was the day a small party of Spaniards landed on San Salvador, gave thanks to God, and claimed the island for the Crown. They were met by wondering Tainos (TI-noes), an Arawak tribe, who seemed to regard them as gods. Christopher Columbus noted in his journal that "they were a gentle and peaceful people and of great simplicity." He gave them "little red caps and glass beads . . . and other things of slight worth." Overcome with gratitude, the Tainos promptly carried out requests to supply food, water, and firewood. Columbus noted thoughtfully, "They should be good servants. . . ."

From then on the Indians had no chance. Their very characteristics brought out the worst in the Spaniards. "These people are very unskilled in arms," Columbus wrote two days later. "With 50 men they all could be subjugated. . . ." When his party left San Salvador, six Indians were taken along.

For Columbus was not just an explorer. He wanted more out of this trip than the thrill of seeing what no white man had seen before. He had insisted on certain conditions before agreeing to lead an expedition westward in search of the Indies. He was to be called Admiral "of all the islands and continents" he might discover or conquer; to be Viceroy and Governor General of all such lands; to receive ten percent of the value of all trade with Spain in products of those lands. Honor, power, and profit made up his personal goal. To that end the Indians now would be expected to contribute.

In fairness to Columbus, his thoughts largely mirrored those of other Europeans of the time. After the long sleep of the Middle Ages, the continent was waking to the age of exploration and the vast returns it promised. The Portuguese Crown already was reaping a harvest from expeditions around Africa to India. The Spanish Crown expected much of Columbus, and he wanted appropriate rewards.

During his first voyage he went on to find and name several other small islands of the Bahamas. Turning southward, he touched at Cuba (where he became the first European to see

HOW THE SPANIARDS CAME   31

tobacco smoked) and the island he called Española, later anglicized to Hispaniola. There on Christmas Eve a ship's boy, unwisely entrusted with the helm, let the *Santa María* run aground. The ship had to be abandoned. With too many men for the remaining space aboard, Columbus decided to use the ship's timbers to build a fort—christened La Navidad (Na-ve-DAHD), which means Christmas in Spanish—and leave about 40 men there.

Columbus then sailed home to announce his wondrous discoveries and display samples of island loot: gold, cotton, strange animals, captured Indians. Word spread gradually through Spain and then across Europe. Spain's rulers heaped honors on the Admiral and urged him to get another expedition ready.

The Crown also went about securing its right to Columbus's discoveries. Europe then was almost entirely Catholic, so the Pope's approval was essential. The desired word came in May 1493, only seven months after the San Salvador landing. Spain was given all lands west of a line about 300 miles west of the Azores Islands in the eastern Atlantic—in effect, the whole Western Hemisphere. Portugal objected strongly, so two years later a new agreement was reached. Known as the Treaty of Tordesillas (Tor-day-SE-yahss), it moved the line another 800 miles west. Portugal thus was allowed to claim the huge eastward bulge of South America now called Brazil.

While Europeans parceled out the property of millions of Indians (who of course knew nothing about it), Columbus was extending his explorations and naming islands right and left. He began his second voyage in 1493 with 1,500 men. They sailed to Dominica and Guadeloupe in the Lesser Antilles, the Virgin Islands and Puerto Rico, Jamaica, some smaller islands, and Cuba's south coast. Columbus also revisited Fort Navidad. In his absence it had been burned and its garrison killed or dispersed. Evidently the Spaniards had treated the local Arawaks badly and the Arawaks, for once, had fought back.

Columbus decided to try again. Eastward along Hispaniola's north coast, in what now is the Dominican Republic, he founded a town called Isabela (for Spain's queen) and placed his brother in charge while Columbus sailed farther. Five months later he

Arawak huts once used throughout the Antilles must have looked much like this reconstruction. It shows typical framing, palm thatch, a stone fireplace—plus modern lights and litter basket.

HOW THE SPANIARDS CAME   33

returned to find that the colonists had been mistreating the Indians, making the latter rebellious. Columbus restored order by various measures, including the use of hunting dogs to chase down Indians. He also sent off five shiploads of them to be sold as slaves in Spain.

On his third voyage Columbus skirted the Caribbean coast of South America. He sighted an island with three peaks and named it Trinidad, meaning trinity. He went ashore in what now is Venezuela. Then he sailed once more to Hispaniola. The colonists had abandoned Isabela, partly because they had seen enough little gold *zemi* statues to convince them that the south coast would yield riches. There they had established a settlement called Santo Domingo.

Santo Domingo was the first permanent European settlement in the New World. It became the capital of Hispaniola, Spain's first American colony. Its basic plan set the pattern for other Spanish towns from Cuba to Chile to California. Typical features are a central plaza dominated by a municipal building and a cathedral (symbols respectively of earthly and spiritual power), a surrounding grid of straight, narrow streets, and a fortified wall.

Unfortunately for Columbus, the early activity at Santo Domingo was less productive than had been expected. Some of the colonists complained that the Admiral was self-seeking and a poor administrator. Back in Madrid, sour remarks were made by noblemen and others who resented the many honors Columbus had received. The Crown heard the growing criticism and decided to send a new governor, Francisco Bobadilla (Bo-ba-DE-ya), to Hispaniola. He was not only to replace Columbus but to judge the latter's behavior. Bobadilla's judgment was that the Admiral should be sent home in chains.

Once home, Columbus soon convinced the Crown that he had been wronged. The chains came off, new honors were proffered, Bobadilla was recalled, and a new governor was sent out.

Everything, in short, seemed all right again. But one big thing had changed: Columbus no longer enjoyed authority over any New World lands. By naming Bobadilla governor, the Crown had assumed direct control over Hispaniola. Henceforth the same system would prevail everywhere.

34   HELLO, WEST INDIES

Colonies now were being set up in fast succession. Columbus on his fourth and last voyage (1502) traversed the coast of Central America and tried to plant several settlements. (His health was failing, and he died in Spain four years later.) Other expeditions meanwhile moved westward in a growing stream, some first to Hispaniola, others direct to more distant points.

The energy and drive of the Spaniards in this period are almost beyond belief. They crossed an uncharted ocean in small, slow, overcrowded, and underprovisioned vessels. They came finally to an alien continent, full of mystery and danger. They faced Indians who soon turned from friendship to bitter hostility. Nothing stopped them. In 1508–11, Puerto Rico was conquered and Jamaica settled. In 1511–15, Cuba was conquered and La Habana founded. In 1509–14, Panama was settled. In 1530, Trinidad was partly occupied. Meanwhile, on the mainland, Mexico, Guatemala, and Peru were subjugated; Florida and Venezuela were colonized, and expeditions ranged as far south as Argentina.

The other side of this extraordinary record is what it did to the Indians. For the gentle Arawaks the outcome was brutally blunt: in less than a century, thanks to forced labor, disease, and outright slaughter, they virtually ceased to exist.*

That was not official Spanish policy. The Crown regarded the Indians as its wards and was concerned for their souls. They were to be subdued peaceably, converted to Christianity, given land, and treated kindly. Every colonizing expedition included priests charged with carrying out these expressed wishes. But they succeeded only partially or not at all.

The main trouble was that Madrid was far away, while the men in the Caribbean—soldiers, adventurers, landowners—had their own ideas. They were after gold, trade, profit. To them the Indians were simply bodies, to be used until they dropped.

"On or near this spot Christopher Columbus landed on the 12th October 1492." So reads the inscription along the base of a big white cross erected to mark the first European landing on San Salvador, Bahamas.

---

* Many died of diseases transmitted by rats, an early import from Europe that soon spread throughout the Antilles. Later, when sugar became a major crop, rats so ravaged the cane that mongooses finally were brought from India to destroy them. Sad to say, the mongooses came to prefer birds and lizards. The rats still are a pest—and so are the mongooses.

36   HELLO, WEST INDIES

Fair-minded churchmen were outraged by this, and some said so out loud. One was Bartolomé de las Casas, who sailed with Columbus on his third voyage and spent most of the next 50 years in the Antilles and Mexico. He agitated for Indian rights on both sides of the Atlantic. (He also favored Negro slavery for a time, then came out strongly against it.) His book, *Destruction of the West Indies,* is an eyewitness account of wholesale torture and murder inflicted by his fellow countrymen on helpless Indians.

Publication of the book met predictable reactions. In Spain some people were horrified. In Spanish America some people cursed Las Casas as a meddler. By and large, brutal treatment of the Indians went right on.

The West Indies produced one exception to this: the Caribs. While the Arawaks let themselves be wiped out, the Caribs resisted so fiercely that the Spaniards generally let them alone. True, the Lesser Antilles (where the Caribs were) offered little to tempt gold-minded conquistadors. But in any case fighting Caribs seemed more trouble than it was worth, and the Spaniards concentrated on exploiting the big islands.

For that they needed labor that could stand long hours in the hot Antillean sun. The Arawaks couldn't. The Caribs wouldn't. But Portugal for some time had been importing occasional African slaves. No doubt Portuguese traders also could ship Africans to Hispaniola?

They could and did. The first load arrived in 1502, and proved a huge success. Bewildered blacks, torn from their native villages and chained for weeks in the hold of a small, stinking ship, emerged to deliver the combination of intelligence and muscle that made them ideal for the job at hand. Soon a clamor rose for more blacks. The authorities responded generously. By 1517, every Spanish resident of Hispaniola could get a license to import ten slaves. Soon they were coming by the thousands.

Thus within a few years of Columbus's first landing the new pattern of West Indian life was set. A handful of Europeans, greedy and well armed, simply erased the original dwellers in paradise. And black men, willy-nilly, began serving white men.

5

OCCUPATION: PIRATE

Spain's rapid expansion into the New World was supposed to be a private affair, but it was impossible to keep it from the neighbors.

The big, echoing news concerned the treasure of Mexico and Peru. Both were homelands of advanced Indian civilizations that for centuries had mined gold, silver, copper, and precious stones, and from them made jewelry, utensils, ornaments, and religious objects. Early expeditions uncovered enough of these to make a conquistador's eyes pop (and a non-Spaniard's ears twitch). By 1530 the shiploads of loot were moving across the Atlantic to Spain. As the ready-made items began to run short, the conquerors put the Indians to work mining ore and smelting it to metal. Meanwhile a continental system of collection and transport was worked out. Eventually it went like this:

From Peru and Ecuador, ships laden with gold, silver, dyewoods, wax, drugs, or other treasure sailed up the Pacific Coast to Panama. There the cargoes were unloaded, packed onto mule trains, and carried across the isthmus to Nombre de Diós (NOME-bray day De-OHSS) or Portobelo on the Caribbean.

From Mexico's mines, metal and precious stones went over the mountains to Veracruz on the Gulf of Mexico. To these were added booty from the Spanish-controlled Philippine Islands, shipped across the Pacific to Acapulco on Mexico's west coast and thence to Veracruz.

From the mountains, valleys, and coastal waters of Venezuela and Colombia came emeralds, gold, and pearls. These were collected in the Caribbean port of Cartagena (Car-ta-HAY-na).

38   HELLO, WEST INDIES

And from Spain each fall came a big fleet that split in two in the Caribbean. Some ships put in at Cartagena, then moved west to Panama. The rest went directly to Veracruz. In spring, bulging with loot, all regrouped at La Habana to prepare for the passage home. They normally set out in early summer and moved northeast with the Gulf Stream past Florida and the Bahamas, then east across the Atlantic.

Using this generally efficient system, Spain took several billion dollars' worth of treasure from the New World in three centuries of colonial power. Though very little of it originated in the West Indies, practically all of it funneled through La Habana. Like a moon rocket in orbit before it is propelled into space, the treasure fleets used the islands as a launching stage before committing themselves to the open ocean.

The reason for this cautious preparation was, in a word, pirates.

Spain claimed as her exclusive property the whole area from the Lesser Antilles to Mexico and Panama, and from Venezuela to the Bahamas. No one else had any legal right there. So said the Treaty of Tordesillas, and Portugal agreed.

The main other European sea powers—France, Holland, and England—felt otherwise. They bristled at a treaty that divided half the world between Portugal and Spain. They condemned (at first) the Spanish treatment of the Indians and the growing slave traffic. Above all, they itched to share Spain's newfound wealth. Since Spain had no intention of sharing anything, the others decided to take some of it away from her.

That is how piracy, an occasional occupation through earlier centuries, won official sanction as a career.

It began with the issuing of letters of marque—commissions permitting the owners of private vessels to arm them and seize enemy ships and cargo in wartime. Privateers became prominent in the late 1400's when Spain and France were at war. French corsairs attacked Spanish ships in European waters. When Spain began annexing the West Indies, corsairs soon followed. One of them made the first capture of a Spanish treasure ship in 1530.

From that it was only a step to outright piracy. Not bothering to obtain letters of marque, tough-minded captains recruited

OCCUPATION: PIRATE 39

loot-minded crews and stood for the Indies. Strictly illegal, they gradually won more or less open approval from their home governments. For the best part of two centuries they harassed the Spaniards, whether or not their countries were at war with Spain.

Pirate tactics were based on speed and surprise. Their vessels normally were smaller and faster than the carracks, caravels, and other Spanish ships. A favorite tactic was to attack the chosen ship at dawn or dusk, coming up silently from astern. As soon as the pirate vessel was close enough, a wedge would be jammed into the Spaniard's rudder, rendering the ship inoperable. Then the pirates quickly threw grappling hooks to bind the ships together and swarmed over the rail for hand-to-hand combat with cutlasses, dirks, pistols, and the like. The Spaniards fought back bravely; each side knew that prisoners would receive scant mercy. Sometimes the pirates were repulsed with losses. Sometimes they captured ship and cargo.

The Spaniards soon improved their vessels, but so did the pirates. Bold raiders would follow a fleet like wolves after cattle. Stragglers might be picked off, a single ship was in constant peril, and some pirates unhesitatingly attacked fortified ports. In 1540 a corsair entered La Habana harbor and sacked and burned the town. Three years later, Frenchman François Leclerc became the first of several raiders to capture Cartagena, loot it, then sail away.

If the French were the first Caribbean pirates, the English eventually produced the most notorious ones. This came with England's growth as a sea power, climaxed by the defeat of the Spanish Armada in 1588. English rulers increasingly encouraged sea captains to "tweak the King of Spain's beard," and the response was enthusiastic.

John Hawkins, for example, was the first Englishman to enter the West Indian slave trade. In 1562, with the open approval of Queen Elizabeth, he sold 300 blacks in Hispaniola. Next he took a larger cargo to Venezuela and Colombia. Later he served as a rear admiral in the defense against the Armada, and was knighted for it.

Hawkins had a young cousin who cut an even bigger swath. His name was Francis Drake, and he took to sea raiding early

Once Britain's naval bastion in the Caribbean, English Harbour on Antigua knew such salty seadogs as Hood, Rodney, and Nelson. Now it has been restored as a tourist attraction and yachtsmen's haven.

and eagerly. In 1572, aged thirty-two, he sailed his ship *Dragon* to Panama and set up a secret jungle base. From there he attacked Nombre de Diós, raided Portobelo, ambushed a mule train with 30 tons of silver, and returned home a hero. His next vessel, the famous *Golden Hind,* ravaged ports and shipping up the west coast of the Americas and went on to circumnavigate the globe, for which Drake was knighted. He then took a fleet to sack and burn the Spanish port of Vigo, crossed to the Caribbean and captured not only Cartagena but Santo Domingo (both of which the Spaniards had to ransom back), and looted settlements in Florida. Drake served in England's victorious battle against the Armada, then made one last foray into the West Indies. This time he was badly beaten in an attack on San Juan, Puerto Rico, but captured and razed Nombre de Diós in Panama.

John Oxenham, one of Drake's lieutenants, took his own expedition to Panama in 1575. Marching across the isthmus, he built a small vessel and raided Spanish shipping on the Pacific side. The Spaniards, however, caught up with him and had him executed.

Death in fact was the lot of many pirates. Their lives rarely were glamorous or swashbuckling. Most of them were common seamen who had not done well at home (quite a few were criminals), and probably only about one in three ever got back there. Even their leaders rarely made out well. Hawkins died at sea off Puerto Rico; Drake died at sea off Panama; the sadistic Frenchman called L'Ollonais, the only known pirate captain to have made prisoners walk the plank, literally was torn apart by Indians.

The average pirate accepted such risks because of the constant hope of winning wealth. The Dutch admiral Piet Heyn captured an entire Spanish fleet off Cuba in 1628 with a cargo worth more than $5,000,000. The notorious Henry Morgan garnered more than $3,500,000 in one six-year period. Such feats goaded lesser men. By choice they sought ships carrying gold or jewels, but much other loot also brought high returns. The pirates who split the proceeds generally spent their shares quickly on drink and diversion, then had to sign on with another crew and try again.

Diamond Rock looms off the palm-fringed southern coast of Martinique in the French West Indies. Here British besiegers gave the French such trouble that England gratefuly commissioned the rock a warship.

42 HELLO, WEST INDIES

The Spanish hold on much of the West Indies began to loosen by the early 1600's. Pirate harassment played a part, but more important was the almost total lack of treasure on the islands as compared to the mainland. Too, Spain's colonial empire was just too big for equal attention to every part of it, particularly with wars regularly breaking out in Europe. In sum, other powers now had the chance to snatch not only at Spanish shipping but also at Spanish islands.

England tried first, in 1624, on St. Christopher (now called St. Kitts) in the Lesser Antilles some 200 miles southeast of Puerto Rico. A French ship put in at St. Kitts the next year, and the English let the newcomers stay because there were Caribs on the island. Together the Europeans got rid of them, only to be sent packing in turn when a Spanish fleet appeared. But after the Spaniards left, some of the English and French returned. Sharing the island amicably—for a while—they made it the first permanent non-Spanish colony in the Antilles.

Meanwhile, some of the French ousted from St. Kitts kept going westward until they reached a little island off the northwest coast of Hispaniola. Columbus had named it Tortuga, meaning turtle, because of its shape. Now it had become the refuge of adventurers and renegades from many lands who called themselves the Brethren of the Coast. Living off the land, Indian fashion, they enjoyed a rough-and-ready democracy which produced, among other things, two famous words.

One came from the Dutch *frei-bote,* a craft sailed by some Dutch Brethren. With a Spanish ending, such a sailor became a *freibotero*—in English, freebooter. The other was a French term for a man who dried meat over a fire called a *boucan;* he was a *boucanier*—in English, buccaneer. Both words went far beyond their original meanings when the Brethren finally were driven off Tortuga and some of them turned to piracy.

By then it was late in the 1600's and the biggest name in pirate circles was that of tough, hard-drinking Henry Morgan. He was one of the roving buccaneers who lent a hand in 1655 when England took a major prize, Jamaica, from the Spaniards. (An attempt on Hispaniola had failed, but Jamaica was sparsely settled and soon captured.) Morgan lived on Jamaica seven years,

OCCUPATION: PIRATE 43

making intermittent raids on Cuba and other Spanish territory. Then he became "respectable" by winning a privateer's commission. Thus equipped, he took part in expeditions that terrorized Spanish ports throughout the Antilles. The high point was a raid on the City of Panama, across the isthmus, that yielded a pack train of 200 mules laden with gold and silver.

When England and Spain signed a treaty halting piracy in the West Indies, Morgan was sent home a prisoner with prospects of being executed. However, his convivial ways and the obvious approval of the Crown combined to win him friends and freedom— topped by knighthood. He went back to Jamaica and became one of the few noted pirates to die in his own bed.

English occupation of Jamaica followed moves into several lesser islands: Barbados, Nevis, Antigua, Montserrat. Meanwhile the French had expanded from St. Kitts to Guadeloupe, Martinique, and elsewhere. The Dutch entered the scene in 1634, occupying altogether six small islands. Even Denmark and Sweden acquired Caribbean footholds, the former in the Virgin Islands and the latter eastward on tiny St. Barthélemy (Bar-tay-leh-ME). All these outposts were in the Lesser Antilles, largely disregarded by the Spaniards. Clearly, things were changing in the Caribbean.

One thing kept up: Spain's flow of wealth from the mainland. But now the treasure fleets were safer than in earlier days. Ships and defensive weapons had been improved. And the European powers no longer condoned piracy. For one thing, pirates had begun attacking ships of all nations, indiscriminately. For another, Spain had decided to commission privateers to protect her fleets —and the privateers went on to raid the ships of other powers, notably England. Henry Morgan actually complained of the "unneighborliness of the Spaniards, who take all our ships at sea or in port. . . ."

During Morgan's heyday, Port Royal, Jamaica, won world notoriety as a pirate haunt and a town of great depravity. Clergymen called it Sin City and predicted dire things. Their predictions came true after Morgan's death, when an earthquake slid Port Royal into the sea.

Thereafter the remaining pirates—and the thieves, deserters, and other hangers-on the profession now attracted—found a ref-

44 HELLO, WEST INDIES

uge northward among the myriad cays of the Bahamas. England had annexed those sparsely settled, largely uncharted islands, and the pirates felt that England still approved of them. After all, an Englishman named Woodes Rogers had just raided his way around the world and brought home a million pounds in loot.

But the British Crown sprang a surprise. Evidently on the theory that it takes a thief to catch one, the same Rogers was named governor of the Bahamas. He served two terms and devoted most of them to rooting out the pirates. Some he recruited into his own honor guard; some he hanged. The rest acknowledged that piracy in those waters really had no future, and either quit or moved elsewhere. By 1730 piracy was as good as finished in the West Indies.

Sea warfare from then on was more conventional, involving naval units. Most of them belonged to England or France, which had become competing colonial powers. They fought each other in Europe and overseas, and sometimes other countries were drawn in. Sometimes the strife centered in the Caribbean, where England established a major fortress on St. Kitts and a matching naval base on Antigua (where a young captain named Horatio Nelson was stationed from 1784 to 1787) while the French were entrenched on Guadeloupe and Martinique.

The decisive years of conflict lasted from about 1755 to 1815. The West Indies were particularly involved three different times.

First was the Seven Years' War (1755–63). Growing out of boundary disputes in North America, it led to fighting over much of the globe. The English generally won. In the West Indies, Admiral Sir George Rodney forced the surrender of the French islands. Most were returned in the peace settlement—which, however, cost France all claim to Canada.

Second was the American Revolution. France, then Spain, then Holland supported the colonials. The British lost the war, but won a crucial naval engagement in the West Indies in 1782. This was the Battle of the Saintes Islands off Guadeloupe, with Admiral Rodney (again) drubbing a French fleet under Admiral Comte de Grasse. The victory secured British sea power in the Caribbean.

Third was the period of Napoleon's march across Europe,

Relics of pirate days, these handsome table items were recovered from the ruins of Port Royal, onetime "sin city" of Jamaica. They include pewter plates and spoons along with china plates and cups.

when Britain took the lead in cutting him down. Among other moves, British warships blockaded the French in the Antilles. French supply ships were spotted sneaking through a narrow channel behind Diamond Rock, a tiny conical islet just off the south coast of Martinique. British sailors under Commodore Sir Samuel Hood managed to scale the high, precipitous Rock and haul up heavy cannon. For a year and a half, until a powerful French fleet dislodged them, they made the channel unusable. Britain was so proud of them that the islet was commissioned a sloop of war, H.M.S. *Diamond Rock*. Passing British naval vessels salute it to this day.

It was in the struggle against Napoleon that Horatio Nelson, the onetime young officer of Antigua, won a place among Britain's seagoing immortals. His victory over a combined French and Spanish fleet at the bloody Battle of Trafalgar, Spain, broke France's naval power. Nelson died of wounds suffered in the fight, but he made England supreme on the world's oceans. And he completed the job the privateers had started three centuries before. Henceforth, ships of any nation could sail freely in the West Indies.

6

MEET THE PLANTOCRATS

Though the more footloose Spaniards left the West Indies early for the mainland, others stayed put. These were the ones who realized that they could get choice land for nothing, develop it with free labor, and settle down in a beautiful climate. They were the start of the island plantocracy—the "aristocracy" that lived on plantations (in Spanish, haciendas).

Some Spanish plantocrats were real aristocrats, members of noble families. More were not. With lands and slaves, however, every man could be a country gentleman. The descendants of such settlers acquired the name *criollo* (cre-O-yo) or creole. It distinguished those of pure white blood (or who claimed to be) from the ever larger number of those with some admixture of other stock, mainly African.

Some haciendas belonged to *peninsulares* born in Spain, actually the ruling class throughout Spanish America. That fact galled the *criollos* increasingly and helped bring on the uprisings that broke Spain's colonial power in the early 1800's. For three centuries, though, life in the Indies rolled on placidly under the hacienda system.

An island hacienda normally covered hundreds or even thousands of acres. Most of this was given over to planting, grazing, or both. The center of operations was the owner's house, modest at first but gradually enlarged as his family grew and he became more prosperous. (Eventually, many houses resembled small castles.) It was built in Spanish style, modified for the tropics. Thick walls of stone or brick, painted white or a pastel shade,

MEET THE PLANTOCRATS   47

supported a red tile roof. Iron grillwork protected windows and decorated balconies. Inside, floors were tiled or of polished wood; furniture tended to be heavy and severe. The house was located and laid out to catch as much as possible of the prevailing wind. The kitchen normally was separate, so that the heat of cooking over big wood fires would not annoy the *hacendado* and his family.

Around the house were workshops to handle construction, repairs, and maintenance. The sawmill, for example, produced lumber from the hacienda's trees, and craftsmen converted some of it to furniture. Hides from hacienda cattle, carefully tanned, became saddles, harness, and shoes. Clothing might be woven from hacienda cotton or the wool of hacienda goats, and dyed with home-grown colorings. So rich was the land, and so varied its products, that an organized hacienda needed virtually nothing from outside. Its work force received food, shelter, clothing, and often some religious instruction—but no cash.

A functioning hacienda could be compared to the feudal domain of a nobleman in the Middle Ages. Its way of life enriched a few and kept everyone else in poverty. And it was truly insular. Ownership of land and slaves passed from father to son. Each new generation tried to build on its inherited wealth. It had few interests beyond the hacienda. World events went by almost unnoticed. The *hacendado* family might visit about, even travel "home" to Spain, but its real home was the hacienda.

The system took root in every colony, though not always equally. In Cuba, as late as 1955, about 1.5 percent of the people owned 46 percent of the land. (This situation helped bring on Fidel Castro.) In Puerto Rico, by contrast, relatively few haciendas ever were set up. Smaller farms, worked by the men who owned them, were more common. (This is one reason why Puerto Rico has not had a Castro.) There were big plantations on Hispaniola, particularly in the remarkably fertile Cibao (Se-BOUGH) Valley of today's Dominican Republic. On Jamaica, vast holdings were portioned out to a few landowners and largely used as open range for cattle and horses. On Trinidad, the Spaniards never expanded much beyond a few coastal settlements.

Many towns on the Spanish islands were just that: settlements.

Few plantocrats' great houses have survived intact from the days when sugar was king in the Caribbean, but this one still stands on French Guadeloupe. And the TV antenna shows it still is lived in.

Except as a seat of government, a town served few needs where most people were bound to plantation life. The main ports gradually grew with trade. Through them passed hacienda exports for Spain, and return cargoes of manufactured goods—furnishings, guns, tools, and so on. The colonies were forbidden to trade with any other nation, or with one another, so smuggling flourished and also helped the ports to grow. In a few the transatlantic treasure fleets gave work to shipwrights, armorers, and the like, along with the workmen who built such massive forts as those of La Habana and San Juan.

The first important island crops were native: tobacco, cacao (source of chocolate), cotton. Then came some from other tropical areas, including rice, coffee, various fruits, and plants that would yield dyes for the expanding cloth makers of Europe.

And then came sugar.

Sugarcane, a member of the grass family, has been known to man for many centuries. The individual stalks or canes grow about six to 12 feet tall. Light green, topped when ripe by a feathery, grayish-tan blossom called an arrow, they contain a sweet

MEET THE PLANTOCRATS   49

juice that can be squeezed out, evaporated to form syrup, then crystallized into sugar. The refining process also produces thick, dark molasses; both molasses and sugar can be used to make rum. Most varieties of cane do best in a warm, moist climate. The West Indies certainly have that.

When the Spaniards came, the Indies had another advantage. Sugar was relatively new to Europe, and wildly popular. A little was being grown in Sicily and southern Spain, which could come nowhere near filling the potential demand. The Indies offered the prospects of almost unlimited markets—and profits.

Sugar was introduced to Hispaniola in 1494. Cultivation began within a few years and shortly spread to Cuba, Puerto Rico, and elsewhere. Endless slave labor let the *hacendados* turn thousands of square miles of forest and savanna into canefields. Eventually cane covered nearly half of the Spanish Antilles' total area. Every island was dotted with stone mills to press the harvested stalks. Wind-driven rollers squeezed out the juice, which was thickened in big kettles over open fires fueled by bagasse (the cane refuse). The juice was cooled in wooden trays that let the molasses drip through. What remained was raw brown sugar.

Later came the *central* (Sen-TRAHL) or sugar factory, coordinated for efficiency. One *central* could handle the cane from many fields, extracting, purifying, and processing the juice to white sugar, with molasses as a by-product.

Spain's success with sugar was a major spur to other Caribbean colonizers. The Dutch, who had learned about sugar in the East Indies, brought their knowledge to the Antilles. Reportedly they introduced cane to both the English (on Barbados in 1637) and the French (on Martinique in 1639). The Dutch also tried it on their own islands, but those proved unsuitable. In any case, the English and French soon were as deep into sugar as the Spaniards, with much the same results. The English, who once had condemned the Spanish slave trade, forced convicts to work the canefields, then turned to full-scale importing of Africans. The French were just as bad. Bewitched by sugar, they felt they had the better of the deal when in the 1763 Treaty of Paris they surrendered all claim to Canada but kept the 687-square-mile island of Guadeloupe.

50 HELLO, WEST INDIES

The new colonizers settled comfortably into the feudal pattern set by the Spaniards. As sugar profits mounted, they began erecting great houses modeled after English or French country homes. A typical mansion might have a long entrance drive under flowering trees, opening to a circle at the porticoed front door. There, slaves in livery took the visitor's mount or carriage and others announced his presence within. While awaiting his host, he might admire vine-shaded verandas and formal gardens, perhaps with a panorama of sea or mountain in the background.

Inside the house would be large, high-ceilinged rooms with floors of gleaming hardwood or marble, walls covered in brocade or paneled in rare woods, velvet hangings, glittering candelabra, bowls of fresh flowers. If the occasion was a dinner party, the service would be of silver, china handmade in Europe, napery of fine damask, food prepared by a trained chef. Slaves would serve the many courses, keep the wine glasses filled, and jump to fill any request.

This kind of ostentation carried over into clothing, jewelry, horses, carriages—anything that could be displayed as proof of one's remarkable good fortune. Some colonials took added pleasure in showing off in Europe. England's King George III, sojourning at the ultrafashionable resort of Bath, once was taken aback when his coach and four were outshone by those of a visiting West Indian.

Sugar even enriched some who never set foot in the Antilles. These were investors who put up money to finance plantation development. The profits usually were reinvested—increasingly, in the latter 1700's, in the new mining and factory enterprises that marked the start of the Industrial Revolution in Europe.

Clearly, sugar was one of the greatest economic bonanzas ever recorded. But in human terms it was ruinous. It depended utterly on slavery. Slavery of course was not invented for that purpose, nor by evil white men. Many peoples had kept slaves in many parts of the world long before Columbus. But slavery in the West Indies nourished a way of life almost as bad for the whites as for the blacks.

Probably its most obvious bad effect was to make landowners see everything in monetary terms. They could not afford to do

MEET THE PLANTOCRATS 51

otherwise. Had they questioned the beauty of profits, they would have questioned the system that made profits possible. But if it was wrong to keep slaves, how could one possibly survive without them? It was too much for most plantocrats even to consider.

By the same token, whites let themselves be supported by the very human beings they were exploiting. Slaves came to do more and more of their work. If an estate was close to self-sufficient, it usually was the slaves who made it so. This could spell security, sometimes freedom, for the capable slave. But it could turn his master into an incompetent parasite.

Then there was the constant contact between slaves and owners. A plantocrat hardly could be born, nursed, fed, bathed, dressed, or even die without blacks at his side. This had various effects. Within a generation, for example, most whites tended to speak their own tongues as their slaves did. An English noblewoman visiting Jamaica noted in her diary that a Jamaican lady of good family (both her parents English) had come to dine. The hostess, making conversation, remarked on the refreshing breeze. "Yaiss, ma'am," the guest responded. "Him really *too* fraish."

But the main result of closeness was the number of children born to white fathers and slave mothers. Often the children were recognized and given the father's name. Many prominent white families ultimately had some Negro blood, and rarely gave it a thought. And it was the relatively high-placed mulattoes who moved toward island leadership when the plantocracy largely bowed out.

That happened at different times in different places, but for one or more of three main reasons:

• Production of sugar from beets (which grow in temperate climates) was improved to the point where it was cheaper for many European consumers than imported cane sugar.

• The Industrial Revolution began to generate capital for use in creating new factories and jobs. Sugar income meant progressively less in Europe, and finally almost nothing.

• Slavery at last was acknowledged to be wrong. In 1807 the slave trade was abolished throughout the British Empire, and emancipation followed. Haiti had been the first Caribbean coun-

52 HELLO, WEST INDIES

try to end slavery when it won independence in 1803. The Dominican Republic was next in 1821. On other islands emancipation came when the colonial powers were ready: Guadeloupe and the Virgin Islands in 1848, Martinique in 1860, the Dutch islands in 1863, Puerto Rico in 1873, and Cuba in 1886.

The end of slavery meant the end of free labor on the haciendas and estates. Added to falling prices for sugar and growing coolness among European investors, it brought on an economic crisis in the West Indies. Now on one island, now on another, the landowners found it harder and harder to make their property pay. Many sold out and left. Some who stayed were able to replace hand labor with machinery, tighten their operations, and keep things going—even turn a profit again. Others changed their cash crop to something else, particularly such fruits as coconuts and bananas. In many cases whites still kept hold of good land generation after generation.

The freed slaves, as we have seen, were poorly prepared to run their own lives. Skilled workers might get jobs, but the big majority of former field hands had only two choices: take up small plots and farm them, or find work on surviving plantations. The adjustment to new conditions was slow and difficult. It is not yet complete.

Nonetheless, the nineteenth century saw the end of the plantocracy and the gradual entry of the West Indies into the modern world.

A restored sugar mill attracts visitors in the United States Virgin Islands. It once had a windvane on top to power the machinery that ground the cane. Ruins of such stone mills dot the West Indies.

7

THE BAHAMAS

Closest of the West Indies to the United States, the Bahama Islands are heavily advertised as an exotic, alluring, yet handy vacation area. Honeyed words and pictures project the message: the Bahamas have a perfect climate, exquisite beaches, crystal-clear water, hotels for every taste and purse, restaurants, night clubs, entertainment, gambling casinos, and on and on and on.

Apparently the advertising works. In 1960, some 340,000 persons visited the Bahamas. Today the yearly total has more than tripled.

The Bahamas' climate is not perfect, of course. Their northwesternmost islands and cays lie only 55 miles off southern Florida. Like Florida, they can get cold northers in winter and rainstorms between May and November. But conditions improve southeastward through the islands, which stretch along the rim of the Atlantic Ocean almost to Haiti, well within the trade-wind belt.

The island themselves would be bigger than Wyoming if they were solid land. As it is, they fill less space than Connecticut. Eight islands or groups make up most of this, with the rest divided among nearly 3,000 cays and rocks big enough to chart. Two islands are more than 100 miles long, one is half as big as Puerto Rico, some are shaped like string beans, others are strung out like beads on a necklace. All are flat: the highest point in the Bahamas is only about 200 feet above sea level.

As this random arrangement suggests, the islands are the visible surface of a vast coral reef built atop underwater mountains.

THE BAHAMAS   55

Much of the reef is just a few feet below the water, forming the extensive Great and Little Bahama Banks that have claimed many ships. Luckily, navigable passages connect the main islands. Two east-west channels cut through from the Atlantic to the Straits of Florida, sending a southern offshoot called the Tongue of the Ocean into the heart of the archipelago. In these channels the bottom drops to depths of a mile or more.

The Bahamas thus include a lot of water and very little land. The water is their main selling point. It displays a palette of colors from cobalt blue (deep) through turquoise and pale green (shallower) to brown (coral bottom) and yellow or white (sand bottom). The water is warm, at least in sheltered areas, all year. And it swarms with creatures offering food, sport, or the fun of observation.

By contrast, the land is not only low but limited. Its surface is weathered coral or fine soil formed by rain and wind. The soil is fertile if it gets enough water, but often it doesn't. Scrubby bushes, palmettos, and tough beach growths are typical island vegetation. Native animals are few, though birds are quite numerous. The native flamingo is the national bird, but the national fruit is the imported pineapple.

The people of the Bahamas are about 85 percent black, almost entirely descended from slaves. The country became an English colony in 1670 and long was run in standard colonial fashion— whites ordering, blacks obeying. This continued after slavery ended in 1838. Whites took over the government in 1964 after Britain gave the colony independence except for foreign affairs and defense. (White-tunicked, pith-helmeted police are the only Bahamian armed force.) The black majority finally won representation in 1967, when a stocky, thirty-six-year-old lawyer named Lynden Pindling became the first Negro prime minister of the Commonwealth of the Bahamas.

Years of largely ignoring black needs are reflected in the people today. Few have had much education. School attendance is compulsory through age fourteen, but there have been too few schools and too many dropouts. Most blacks are church members, but some still believe in chickcharnies (mischievous elves who live in the tops of pine trees). Most enjoy singing and danc-

56 HELLO, WEST INDIES

ing, but they have yet to produce an artist or writer of note.*
While many have taken jobs in white-run resorts, most are torn
between the need for work and the desire to relax by the sea in the
sunshine.

Altogether there are about 160,000 Bahamians. More than
half live on one island, New Providence. Small but central, New
Providence has the only natural deep-water harbor in the Bahamas. It was the logical spot to locate Nassau, the capital.

Nassau retains some colonial charm: old government buildings, frame hotels, comfortable homes, flowers everywhere, and
horse-drawn carriages threading through the auto traffic on Bay
Street, the narrow main artery. Tourists usually are impressed.
They enjoy bargaining for Bahamian handcrafts (chiefly straw
baskets and hats) in the open-air market. After dark they may
sample good restaurants, the gambling casino across the harbor
on Paradise Island (formerly Hog Island), or the "native" night
clubs.

Most of the night clubs are in the section called Over the Hill,
which actually comprises most of Nassau because it is where almost 80,000 blacks live. It is a shamefully poor area, with some
pleasant homes but many slum blocks—crowded, dirty, unsani-
tary. There are too few schools, hospitals, and clinics. From these
sleazy streets the taxi drivers, store clerks, hotel and domestic
servants come out to work, then return to sleep. So do waterfront
loungers, hustlers, and thieves. Prime Minister Pinding was born
in Over the Hill, but he was lucky; his father saw to it that he got
a good education and a chance to move on.

Out from Nassau in all directions lie the other Bahama islands,
logically called the Out Islands. Fewer than 30 are inhabited,
mainly by farmers and fishermen. Small, neat cottages line the
short streets of scattered settlements, and boats are drawn up on

*Visitors to Nassau, capital of the Bahamas, pose with a traffic policeman
alongside a signpost showing distances to the main "out islands." Behind
them is a fringe-topped, horse-drawn carriage.*

* Actor Sidney Poitier attended school in the Bahamas. But he was born in Miami,
Fla.

58 HELLO, WEST INDIES

hundreds of beaches. All the main Out Islands can be reached from Nassau by water or air, and today they are being developed as never before. Starting northwest of Nassau and going clockwise, they fall into seven groups.

Grand Bahama is a resort area carved out of empty scrubland since the 1950's at a cost of roughly half a billion dollars. The main feature is Freeport, a town centered around gambling, hotels, shopping, and restaurants. American visitors often fly over from Florida just for the evening. Freeport's man-made harbor welcomes cruise ships, along with oil-powered cargo vessels that stop by in growing numbers to fuel their tanks by underwater pipeline from the shore. About 25,000 people live on Grand Bahama Island.

Great and Little Abaco combine old and new. There are quaint villages and modern tourist facilities. On one beach, traditional wooden boats are built by hand. Not far away an American company harvests pine pulpwood for making boxes, planting sugarcane after the trees are cut.

Eleuthera was settled in 1648 by religious dissenters from Bermuda. The settlement fared poorly, but later arrivals did better. Their descendants farm Eleuthera's good soil and fish its waters, supplying seafood, vegetables, and fruit to Nassau. On Eleuthera an American tracking station monitors missiles launched from Florida's Cape Kennedy.

The southeastern islands, still largely undeveloped, include some noteworthy features. On Cat Island is Comer Hill, the Bahamas' high point (205 feet), topped by the hermitage of a monk named Father Jerome who built it by hand and lived there until his death. San Salvador Island is where Columbus presumably landed; there is disagreement about the exact spot, so three separate monuments have been erected. Long Island has old colonial great houses and a huge cave with Arawak paintings. Great Inagua Island is inhabited largely by flamingos that breed by thousands under government protection.

The Exuma chain, a long, thin line of islands southeast of Nassau, attracts yachtsmen with its beautiful water and countless sheltered anchorages. The major local event is the Out Island Regatta, held each April at George Town on Great Exuma. This

THE BAHAMAS   59

is a wild series of races for Bahamian working sailboats, which attracts spectators from all over the Bahamas. The boats are not big, rarely over 35 feet, and lack ballast keels. For stability when racing, each carries up to 20 men whose main job is to shift their weight as needed. The packed craft take off all together, and accidents are normal as they careen around the course in pursuit of cash prizes.

Andros, the biggest Bahamian island, was until recently the least developed. It is flat, bare, and largely surrounded by extremely shallow water, but now a large-scale farming development, irrigated by wells, produces fruits and vegetables for markets as far off as Europe. For contrast, there is the undersea weapons range of the U.S. Navy off Andros's east coast, on the edge of the Tongue of the Ocean. The deep water, never entered by ocean vessels, permits testing of the behavior of torpedoes and other weapons over a range of nearly 100 miles.

Bimini and nearby cays are the first land usually sighted by boats coming from Florida. They lie between the Gulf Stream and the Great Bahama Bank, and anglers come from all over the world to fish their teeming waters.

Compared to some parts of the West Indies, the Bahamas have little history. The Spaniards failed to settle there after Columbus; instead, they shipped out some 40,000 Arawaks to work—and die—in the mines of Hispaniola. Thereafter the only important visitor was Ponce de León in 1513, up from Puerto Rico on a futile hunt for the Fountain of Youth.

England eyed the islands in the early 1600's, but took no action until 1670. New Providence then was occupied and Nassau founded, though the settlers were plagued by pirates until Woodes Rogers came to establish order. His success led to what still is the Bahamian motto—*Expulsis Piratis Restituta Commercia* (Pirates Expelled Commerce Restored).

The Spaniards attacked Nassau several times and continued to claim the Bahamas until 1783, when British ownership was settled by treaty. The population meanwhile was growing by several thousand—former American colonials who had remained loyal to the Crown during our revolution came with families, goods, and slaves. A quiet plantocracy was in the making.

THE BAHAMAS   61

The end of slavery brought hard times. Some planters left. Others turned to a new field, the salvage of ships wrecked on the largely unmarked Bahamian banks. Some residents helped things along by moving shore lights to fool passing helmsmen, or making deals with skippers to run aground on purpose. Bahamians did well on salvage until a new governor built a system of lighthouses that ended their game.

The American Civil War yielded a fresh bonanza when the Union blockaded Confederate ports and Nassau became a base for blockade runners. Taking in guns and bringing out cotton to be sent on to England, they made Nassau a temporary boomtown. War's end led to a slump that lasted until the 1920's. Then the American "noble experiment," Prohibition, showed again how handy the Bahamas can be for breaking our laws. This time, rumrunners in high-powered speedboats carried illegal liquor across to Florida, enriching bootleggers and gangsters and creating a new crop of Bahamian millionaires.

The islands' later years have been closely involved with tourism. In the 1930's and 1940's, Nassau emerged as a popular winter resort. It drew wealthy folk who could afford to stay several months and cruise-ship trippers who left after a day or two. Neither group seemed likely to support an economy that had practically no other resources. In 1949 the government began a big campaign to attract tourists the year round.

That year, some 32,000 persons visited the Bahamas. We know what has happened since. The vast upsurge in tourism has done wonders for the country, helped by other developments. New industries have been lured by the fact that there are no Bahamian taxes on incomes, sales, or capital gains. (Most government expenses are met by import duties.) International companies similarly have made Nassau their headquarters. All this has encouraged dozens of American, Canadian, and British banks to open offices there.

A Bahamian workboat named Tida Wave *boils along in a race of the Out Island Regatta off George Town, Great Exuma. The whole crew perches on the port rail to help keep the craft on an even keel.*

62   HELLO, WEST INDIES

Besides such legal moves, some illegal ones have occurred. The details are long and complicated, but basically they involve American and Canadian promoters who were allowed to attract tourists their own way, particularly by opening gambling casinos. Gambling was, and is, against Bahamian law. However, exceptions were made for two casinos an American wanted to build. He received this special treatment largely through the help of a British-born lawyer who was at the same time a government official and a member of the businessmen's group known, from the addresses of their Nassau offices, as the "Bay Street Boys." Others of the Bay Street Boys also were in the government. Among them, they arranged for the American to buy much of Grand Bahama Island for a song and erect the gaudy tourist mecca, Freeport. In return for such kindness the Bay Street Boys received shares in new enterprises or handsome fees. The lawyer was paid more than a million dollars for his help on the casinos.

To top it off, American underworld figures, including the Mafia, got into the gambling picture. All in all, there was good reason for voters to reject the white-dominated United Bahamian Party, to which all the Bay Street Boys belonged, in the 1967 election and, for the first time, give strong support to the largely black Progressive Liberal Party and its leader Lynden Pindling.

Pindling soon showed that the voters had chosen well. While prying the underworld loose from the gambling casinos, he kept the casinos themselves and "cut the government in" by levying a $1,000,000 tax on each. (By law, Bahamian citizens are forbidden to gamble.) They went right on thriving. So did most of the other new businesses, notably banking and construction.

This enabled the government to begin spending money on real Bahamian needs, including education, housing, and health services. When another election was held in 1968, Pindling voted in a brand-new school his government had built on Andros. It appeared that the average islander at last was being fairly treated. But Pindling did not play favorites. When some Bahamians expressed their new self-confidence by being rude to tourists, he launched a campaign to remind all islanders that tourism is their bread and butter.

The nation has close economic ties with the United States, its

THE BAHAMAS   63

chief commercial supplier and best customer. It has abandoned
the British pound for a Bahamian dollar kept at par with ours.
Some Bahamians would like to see the islands an American state.
Most, however, have a clear-cut goal: to run their own country.

The Turks and Caicos Islands

Down at the southeastern end of the Bahamas, geographically
part of them but politically separate, are the hot, dry Turks and
Caicos (KI-koce) Islands. A British colony, they cover only 166
square miles. Most of their 6,000 people fish for a living. The
name Turks comes from a local cactus that bears a fez-shaped
red flower. The largest island, Grand Turk, is six miles long. It
has a U.S. Navy oceanographic base at one end and a U.S. Air
Force missile-tracking station at the other, and the road joining
them is the only paved road in the colony. In the outside world,
the Turks and Caicos Islands probably are best known to stamp
collectors.

José Martí, father of Cuban independence, eyes the camera in this rare photo. Though not a particularly inspiring man physically, Martí stirred the emotions of other Cubans with his forceful words.

8

CUBA

"You want to know what Fidel Castro has done to Cuba? I tell you, he has made it into a new country where life is better for everyone!"

"Let *me* tell you what Castro has done to the Cuba I love. He has ruined it!"

Two Cubans, two points of view: both are partly right and partly wrong. They express the main reactions of people everywhere to what has gone on in Cuba since bearded young Fidel Castro came to power in 1959. For Castro has indeed remade his island nation. He has set great and far-reaching changes in motion. For good or ill, Cuba never again will be as it was before.

How was it before?

To start, Cuba was and is unique in the West Indies. By far the biggest island in size (and population), it stretches farther east and west than the distance from Boston to Detroit. It is more or less mountainous throughout, rising to about 6,000 feet in the southeastern Sierra Maestra (Ma-ES-tra). That range hides mineral deposits, notably nickel, copper, and manganese, unmatched in the Antilles.

But Cuba's main wealth is in the lowlands and rolling valleys that make up more than half her area. Most of this is planted to sugarcane, for which the soil and climate are ideal. Cuba alone could produce a quarter of the sugar the world consumes. It also is famed as a source of fine cigar tobacco.

Cuba is beautiful. The lush green countryside is spangled with rivers and dotted with the tall, graceful royal palm. Tropical flowers and birds add fragrance and color. (Among the birds is the

66   HELLO, WEST INDIES

world's smallest hummingbird, no bigger than a bumblebee.) The capital, La Habana, long has been considered a showplace, blending Spanish colonial architecture with Cuban modern. The old treasure port fronts on a commodious harbor. Newer sections open out with wide boulevards, pastel-colored homes, parks, playgrounds. With the largest population of any island capital (about a million persons), La Habana also has some of the most historic buildings (including the Cathedral, the National Museum, and the Presidential Palace) and some of the tallest ones (including a real skyscraper of 33 stories).

Cuba lies so close to the United States—the north coast is just 90 miles from Key West, Florida—that it has figured in American thinking for centuries. Several times our government came close to annexing it. Before 1959 it drew more American tourists than the rest of the Antilles put together.

In those days Cuba was a republic, at least in name. Actually, a brutal and corrupt dictator, Fulgencio Batista (Fool-HEN-seo Ba-TEES-ta), ran the country largely for the benefit of a small upper class. Most Cubans were poor and uneducated, with little hope of better. This is the classic situation in Latin American countries that have thrown off Spanish rule and found themselves unprepared for democracy. Cuba may have been worse prepared than most because independence came late—five full centuries after Columbus.

The first settlers arrived from Hispaniola in 1514. Finding no gold, they moved on or turned to planting. Large haciendas became the rule. The relative number of slaves, though, was lower than on many islands. Today the population is estimated at 72 percent white, 27 percent Negro and mulatto, and 1 percent Oriental.

In 1515, Santiago de Cuba on the southeast coast became Cuba's capital. It was close to Hispaniola, with a good harbor. But that of La Habana, across the island and some 465 miles west, was better located for the Spaniards' needs, and in 1589 the capital was moved. Immigrants still came in via Santiago—from Jamaica after 1655, when England annexed that island; from Haiti after 1790, when French Créole landowners fled the slave uprisings there.

CUBA 67

La Habana meanwhile became the main rendezvous point for eastbound treasure ships, and fair game for pirates. After various raids the city was captured by an English force in 1762. Spain got it back only in exchange for Florida, and later got Florida back in exchange for the Bahamas.

In the early 1800's, when other Spanish colonies revolted, Cuba stayed loyal. Taking no chances, Spain put the island under martial law and sent out stern governors. One of them exiled Cuba's first important writer, José María Heredia (Eh-RAY-dea), for his political beliefs. Heredia kept writing, but missed his homeland. A visit to Niagara Falls inspired an ode in which he mourned that the cataract was not surrounded by Cuban palms.

Other writers expressed stronger feelings, particularly about slavery. One was Cirilo Villaverda (Ve-ya-VAIR-day), whose novel *Cecilia Valdés* protested the second-class status of Negroes. In 1844 an unsuccessful slave rebellion underscored the point.

Cuban events caused mixed feelings in the United States. Pro-slavery interests wanted to see Cuba annexed as a southern state. Northerners were more concerned over the treatment of Cuba's people. President James Polk offered to buy Cuba for $120,000,-000, but Spain refused. Later, Presidents Pierce and Buchanan also tried to acquire the island.

The American Civil War temporarily ended our interest in Cuba and permanently ended slavery in the United States. Independence-minded Cubans were greatly encouraged. In 1868 a revolution was proclaimed at Yara, in the Sierra Maestra. Fighting continued for ten years before a truce was declared. Spain promised to abolish slavery in Cuba, and finally did so in 1886. But other grievances remained: high taxes, dictatorial Spanish officials, graft and bribery in government. Cubans who complained were likely to be exiled. Some made their way to New York and began planning a new revolution.

The most ardent spokesman of the New York exiles was the poet and journalist José Martí (Mar-TE). Born in La Habana in 1853, he had been exiled for his political leanings while still in his teens. Now he wrote passionately on conditions in Cuba and the need to act on them. The action came in 1895. Revolution again exploded on the island and many exiles rushed to join

68   HELLO, WEST INDIES

in. Martí was one of the first to return—and to fall in action. His death transformed him into the hero of Cuba's fight for freedom, the George Washington of his people.

The fighting continued for three years. The rebels adopted hit-and-run tactics, destroying crops, sugar mills, and railroads. Since a fair amount of the property belonged to Americans, our government watched apprehensively. Then the Spaniards began setting up concentration camps and herding whole villages into them. Many persons died in the camps, and Americans were alarmed about that.

Finally, certain newspapers—the so-called yellow press—demanded war against Spain. President McKinley was opposed, but the public apparently believed the newspaper stories of Spanish "atrocities" and the clamor for intervention grew. Then the battleship *Maine* was ordered to La Habana, chiefly to reassure Americans and American property owners, and on February 15, 1898 the ship was blown up, killing 260 men. To this day no one knows who did it. In March the President urged Spain to declare an armistice in Cuba, and in April the Spanish agreed. Too late. The next day, McKinley asked for a declaration of war.

Three battles ensued. Far off in the Philippines, half the Spanish navy was destroyed in a few hours by an American fleet sent from Hong Kong. Most remaining Spanish ships were bottled up at Santiago de Cuba; when they tried to break out, they were sunk. American troops landed at Santiago and the Spaniards offered little resistance. All told, hostilities lasted less than four months.

This one-sided victory in a largely unjustified war brought the United States some new territories—Puerto Rico, the Philippines, Guam—and the problem of Cuba. As a start, we placed a military government in charge until a Cuban government could be formed. While waiting, our soldiers put in some useful work.

They were concerned about sanitary conditions, which under Spanish rule had been bad indeed. Tropical diseases ravaged Cuba, one of the worst being yellow fever. After years of study, a Cuban doctor named Carlos Finlay had reached the unheard-of conclusion that the fever was transmitted by mosquitoes. Now the army doctors used soldier volunteers to test Finlay's notion, and

This was La Habana in 1955, when Fulgencio Batista ran Cuba. The broad boulevard runs along the Malecón (Ma-lay-CONE), or seawall. In the background are hotels, other buildings, and a radio tower.

found it correct. Soon the culprit, the *Aedes aegypti* mosquito, was brought under control and yellow fever with it.

Cuba's first constitution was drawn up in 1901. Modeled after that of the United States, it provided for the island's first elected government. Our troops withdrew from a cleaner capital. Politically, however, it did not stay clean long. The Cubans had no experience in self-government and handled it sloppily. Graft and bribery flourished; elections brought fraud and violence. Four years after Tomás Estrada Palma became Cuba's first president,

70   HELLO, WEST INDIES

an armed revolt broke out and the United States sent back troops. By 1909 it appeared that elected governments again could take charge. They ruled more or less effectively for 25 years.

This period of relative stability encouraged Cuban creativity. By the 1920's, such varied talents were emerging as Alejo Carpentier, several of whose novels have been translated into English; Nicolás Guillen, poet of strongly African feeling; anthropologist Fernando Ortiz, who called typical Cuban music the result of "the love affair of the Spanish guitar and the African drum"; composers Ernesto Lecuona, Amadeo Roldán, and Joaquín Nin; painters Mario Carreño and Wilfredo Lam; and sculptor Juan José Sicre, whose works may be seen in most countries of the hemisphere.

But the 1920's also were a time of growing political tension. In 1925, General Gerardo Machado took office as president and soon made himself dictator. By 1933 he was so hated that a group of younger army men overthrew him and sent him into exile. Then things got out of hand. Machado's successor lasted one month; *his* successor, four months. A provisional president took office in 1934, but resigned in 1935. His successor was impeached in 1936. Gradually one man emerged from the confusion as Cuba's real boss—Fulgencio Batista.

An army sergeant self-promoted to colonel, Batista ran the country openly or through puppet presidents for 20-odd years. He never won popular support, although, interestingly (in view of what happened later,) he long was backed by the Cuban Communist Party. Elected president in 1940, he took Cuba into World War II on the Allied side. Then he let two hand-picked successors hold office. Their terms were marked by growing prosperity, but also by graft and corruption at every level of government.

In 1952, with a presidential election scheduled, Batista decided simply to take over. Henceforth he was openly a dictator, quick to punish critics and reward supporters. On one hand, he had an estimated 20,000 persons murdered and countless others maimed or jailed. On the other hand, he gave Cuba a building boom—mostly in La Habana, and particularly in the form of hotels and gambling casinos. Rich Cubans got richer. So did Americans and Canadians who invested in construction, sugar, mining,

CUBA 71

and other opportunities. The delights of La Habana brought tourists flocking. For their benefit many hotels, restaurants, and other public places were racially segregated.

Cuba's middle class profited under Batista. Cubans came to own a majority of the sugar mills and manufacturing firms, and virtually all small businesses. The professional class of doctors, lawyers, and so on was one of the largest in any Latin American country. As more and more people moved into the cities, La Habana alone came to hold one Cuban in five.

Batista prosperity meant little to the laboring class, which included a big majority of the city dwellers and practically all rural residents. The dictator largely ignored the *campesinos* who needed schools, health care, and above all jobs. Sugar production, Cuba's biggest revenue earner, was being increasingly mechanized, boosting profits but throwing men out of work. Hundreds of thousands of *campesinos* worked only a few months a year, while others had no regular jobs. All in all, most Cubans had small reason to love the dictator.

Many hated him. Within a year of his seizing power, several underground groups were after his scalp. The group that got it went on to run the country under Fidel Castro.

Castro was a lawyer by training, a revolutionary by choice. He had been a student agitator at the University of La Habana and a candidate for congress in the canceled 1952 election. The next year, he and a few followers tried to take over the army's Moncada Barracks in Santiago de Cuba. The attempt failed and Castro went to jail. But the date of the raid, July 26, became historic to Fidel's supporters, for it marked the start of his eventual rise to power.

That rise began in 1956, after Castro had been freed and gone to Mexico to organize a fighting force. It was so small that everyone could sail back to Cuba on one yacht, the former property of an American who had named it *Granma*. They landed near Santiago and moved up into the Sierra Maestra. There they began raiding villages and sugar mills, guerrilla style, sometimes clashing with Batista troops. Most people in the area favored Castro's campaign. Elsewhere on the island other groups were active, and gradually Batista lost control. After his army was defeated in

72   HELLO, WEST INDIES

several pitched battles, he gave up. On January 1, 1959 he left Cuba for keeps.

Of all Batista's opponents, Castro was best prepared to replace him. The bearded revolutionary promptly did so. He promised free elections, free speech, and a free press. Cubans and Americans welcomed the prospects.

What Castro then gave his country was something else. He let Batista's political prisoners out of jail, executed some of the people who had put them there, then imprisoned a considerably larger number of Cubans who criticized *him*. He put off elections indefinitely. He took over the press and made it into a propaganda vehicle. In less than a year he had dropped any pretense of democracy in favor of a communist-style dictatorship. This was the recommendation of Castro's two closest advisers, his brother Raul and Ernesto "Che" Guevara (Gay-VA-ra), an Argentine doctor who had cast his lot with the *fidelista* revolution.

A communist regime 90 miles from Florida was, of course, a major concern to the United States. Our government first tried to talk Castro out of it. That failing, we halted all trade with Cuba, closing her main sugar market. The Soviet Union then announced that it would buy the sugar, give Cuba economic aid (later estimated at about $1,000,000 a day), and defend Cuba in case of attack—presumably from the U.S. or our naval base (under perpetual lease since 1934) at Guantánamo near Cuba's eastern tip.

Castro meanwhile was remaking Cuban life. He seized all the sugar plantations, gave some of the land to *campesinos,* and organized the rest into state-owned collective farms. Manufacturing and trade went the same way. American property worth hundreds of millions of dollars was taken without compensation. Cuban owners and managers were powerless. Those who objected were jailed or exiled. Soon, many were choosing exile voluntarily.

Most of them flew to Miami in airplanes supplied by our government. The rush to get out created a backlog of Cubans who waited as long as three years for plane seats. Castro called them *gusanos* or worms, and treated them accordingly. When a man applied for permission to leave, he was fired from his job and forbidden to withdraw money from the bank. His survival thereafter was up to him.

After a dozen years of Castro, more than half a million Cubans had fled their homeland and a great many more wanted to. Among them were most of the country's educated business, professional, and technical men. In Miami alone the Cuban "colony" numbered close to 400,000 persons. Many became American citizens and settled down to stay.

A happy Fidel Castro stands beside bereted "Che" Guevara and Soviet official Anastas Mikoyan in this 1963 photo. Today Mikoyan has been retired, Guevara is dead, and Castro probably has less to smile about.

74   HELLO, WEST INDIES

But others lived in hopes of return, and many plots against Castro were laid. The United States got involved in one of them, in 1961, when some 1,400 exiles tried to land at the Bay of Pigs on the island's swampy south coast. The Cubans had been trained and equipped by our government, but they were met by Castro troops and soundly defeated.

In 1962 came a more serious confrontation, involving the Soviet Union. Secretly, Russia had begun sending intermediate-range missiles to Cuba and thousands of technicians to oversee launching sites for them. Every site was aimed at the United States. When our government learned of this, President Kennedy reached a firm conclusion: the missiles must go. Otherwise, war between Russia and America might erupt. Kennedy so notified the Soviet government, and after tense hours of waiting his demand was accepted.

Castro publicly criticized Russia over this. Indeed, his early successes made him cocky. Trying to "export" revolution to other Latin American countries, he set up shortwave radio stations to broadcast propaganda—most of it violently anti-American—throughout the hemisphere. He went on to train and equip forces dedicated to the overthrow of the governments of Venezuela, Bolivia, and other nations. The Organization of American States dropped Cuba from membership, and later almost every country in the hemisphere severed relations with Cuba. Unimpressed, Castro went on trying to export revolution.

His most spectacular try, and failure, came in 1967. His friend Che Guevara evidently had decided that the impoverished Indians of Bolivia were ripe for revolt. Guevara and a dozen Cuban army officers went to Bolivia, recruited guerrillas, and undertook the kind of action that had worked in the Sierra Maestra. It was a bad miscalculation. The Indians spurned them, deserters revealed Che's plans to the Bolivian army, the would-be revolutionaries ran out of food and water, and Guevara was captured and shot. This clumsy performance made him an instant hero in Cuba. (And some other places. One was Bolivia's southern neighbor, Chile, where the Marxist government elected in 1970 promptly reestablished relations with Cuba).

On the home front Castro faced problems. One of the biggest

CUBA 75

was the shortage of consumer goods brought on by the American economic blockade. Rationing of food, clothing, and other things began in 1961 and grew steadily tighter. Castro first tried to ease this by setting up factories, but settled for increased sugar production to boost export income.

That in turn created headaches, partly because of a sudden lack of manpower. Many *campesinos* had found work on new state projects, leaving too few to harvest the cane each year. Castro's solution was to send out thousands of "volunteer" cutters, from prisoners and soldiers to students and office workers. A few genuine volunteers came from other countries, including both Russia and the United States.

Even with big harvests, however, Cuba still had to import food. Castro found a partial answer in a new program of cattle breeding. Hybrid animals adapted to the Cuban climate promised more beef for Cuban tables. At the same time, Castro decreed that a 100,000-acre "green belt" around La Habana be cleared and planted with citrus, coffee, and other food crops.

Fidel's concern for the producing countryside was matched by his decreasing interest in the cities. La Habana in particular was becoming an echo of its glittering, prosperous self. Streets were nearly empty because of gasoline rationing. Office buildings housed the mushrooming staffs of government planners. With most restaurants and other public places closed, the most popular spot in any city was likely to be the Coppelia ice-cream parlor, a state enterprise dispensing 50-odd flavors.

The state now told almost every Cuban where to work, when, and for what pay. Many people obeyed because they had no choice. But many sincerely believed that the revolution was improving their lives. In some cases they undoubtedly were right.

For one thing, official segregation of Negroes had been halted. Most blacks were grateful to Castro for that.

Women, too, were getting more freedom. Men in Latin American lands traditionally handle important matters and leave women to run the home. In Cuba under Castro women could step out and take jobs, even if only those the state approved.

Public health received far more attention than under Batista. So did housing needs. As for education, hundreds of new schools

76 HELLO, WEST INDIES

were built and thousands of new teachers were trained. Television became a major instructional tool. Secondary schooling now was concentrated in the cities, above all La Habana. There, scores of mansions that had belonged to well-to-do families were made into living quarters for students sent to the capital to study on state scholarships. More young people now could go on to college and other advanced schooling. At all levels, they received considerable propaganda with their studies.

Propaganda of course has been an important tool for Castro. In 1959, La Habana boasted 16 daily newspapers, some of high caliber. Within a short time there were just two, both communist-oriented (one named *Granma* for Castro's invasion yacht). Radio and television similarly were taken over. Culture was made to serve the revolution, as when a good artist was hailed as a good *socialist* artist.

Even sports helped the cause. People of all ages were urged to participate in order to grow strong, clean, and better prepared for the great anti-imperalist struggle. They also were told that professional sports were capitalistic and must cease. This particularly hit baseball, long the national game. Once Cuba had produced thousands of able players, hundreds of professionals, and dozens of American big-leaguers. La Habana had had a team in the top-level minor league, the International. When it won the Little World Series in 1959, Castro himself was cheering in the stands. But once in power he decided that no one should compete for money, so professional baseball, along with soccer, *jai alai,* prize-fighting, and horse racing, came to an end.

In broad terms, Castro seemed to be helping some groups—the poor, the Negroes, the young—at the expense of the well-off and those who believed in such things as private ownership and a competitive economy. This is the classic pattern of communism. In Cuba it was to go further, into the area of human thought and behavior. Castro's announced aim was to give the nation a "new morality," even to create a "new Cuban." Apparently this would be a person of high motives and dedication, eager to work endlessly for his country's good (as defined by Fidel) without thought of personal reward.

How far such ideas might succeed remained to be seen. Castro

CUBA 77

obviously had strong support, strong enough to survive, for example, the failure of his boastful campaign to harvest 10,000,000 tons of sugar in 1970. (The crop fell about 1,500,000 tons short.) Perhaps the "new Cuban" was tiring after years of hard work for few visible rewards. In 1971, Castro admitted publicly that Cuba still faced big problems, including a labor shortage, decreasing output per worker, tighter rationing, and an astonishing figure of some 400,000 boys and girls under 16 who had dropped out of school and were not working.

The balance sheet on Castro will take a while to figure. As this is written, he remains in power and his prospects are mixed.

9

JAMAICA

Like a big green turtle, Jamaica floats in the Caribbean some 90 miles south of eastern Cuba and 550 miles north of Panama. Its area, almost identical with that of the numerous Bahamas, makes it the third largest of the Greater Antilles. Its central spine rises steeply to more than 7,000 feet in the eastern jumble of the Blue Mountains. A narrow coastal plain, widening to about 30 miles in spots, rims most of the island.

The Arawaks called it Xamayca, apparently meaning "Land of Streams." Columbus sighted it in 1494. It was colonized from Hispaniola in 1510, then almost forgotten until the English seized it a century and a half later. (There then were perhaps 2,000 Spanish *criollos* on the whole island.) The new owners built up a rich sugar plantocracy. After slavery ended in 1838 the island went into a long economic decline.

Biggest of Britain's Antillean territories, Jamaica in 1962 became the first to gain independence within the Commonwealth. Since then its approximately two million people, 92 percent black or mulatto, have gone it alone.

To visitors, Jamaica is a vacation eden. They praise its fine beaches and lush landscape; the string of attractive, if expensive, hotels along the north coast from Montego Bay to Ocho Rios and Port Antonio; the bustle and variety of Kingston, Jamaica's capital on the south coast; and the friendly, warm-hearted people. Jamaica has all that plus a conscientious tourist board. And since it is only three hours by air from New York, with two international airports and full cruise-ship facilities, it deservedly attracts

The Georgian Square in Spanish Town, once Jamaica's capital, blends beautiful English architecture with tropical palms and a manicured lawn. Old cannon still flank the entrance to the building at right.

80 HELLO, WEST INDIES

visitors. Tourism brings in more revenue than sugar, bananas, coconuts, citrus fruits, or any other crop, including the berries of the pimento trees that make Jamaica the world's leading producer of allspice.

Pimento of course is a small earner. By contrast, the island's biggest export is bauxite, the reddish ore from which aluminum is extracted. A thick layer of bauxite covers nearly a quarter of the island's surface. Foreign companies mine it under contract, taking out a quarter of all the bauxite produced in the world. Most of it has gone to the United States or Canada for the two stages of processing: into alumina (aluminum oxide), then metal. Recently Jamaica's first alumina plant was erected.

Visitors become conscious of bauxite if they are driving along the coast and pass a shipment point. There the ore is brought out from the mines by rail or overhead conveyor, and dumped onto waiting vessels. The immediate area is thick with reddish dust, vivid against the green landscape. The government requires mining areas to be refilled, replanted, and used for agriculture. This keeps "dust bowls" from starting. It also has brought such benefits as the largest cattle herd in the Antilles, maintained by an American aluminum company.

Jamaica has other animals, most of which the visitor never sees. Native mammals are small and shy. Nightfall brings out the bats, largely eaters of fruit and insects. They are called rat-bats because butterflies and moths are called bats. (Frogs are called toads, toads are called bullfrogs, and crocodiles are called alligators.) There are more than 100 species of bat, or butterfly, on the island, and 25-odd kinds of rat-bat, or bat. The world's biggest swallowtail butterfly—wingspread more than six inches —lives on Jamaica. So does the streamertail hummingbird, which is green and black with a red bill and a tail more than twice its body length. It is Jamaica's national bird, but Jamaicans don't call it the streamertail hummingbird. They call it the doctor bird.

Like other Antillean islands, Jamaica has problems that stem primarily from the slavery years. So do the people who face those problems.

Jamaica's plantocracy was unusually prosperous. Its great houses dotted the fertile cane land and its members lived like

JAMAICA 81

princes. The 1791 census counted 30,000 Europeans and 250,-000 slaves. It included 10,000 "free people of colour" or mulattoes. When sugar planting declined, many whites left and the mulattoes emerged as the most important group on the island. Ten years after emancipation, they numbered 68,000 as against 15,000 Europeans and 293,000 Africans.

The freed slaves generally wanted to leave the big estates. Most of them moved to more remote areas, often high in the mountains, where they could scratch a living from the soil. When a long drought hit the island in 1864–65, some of them grew restive. The British authorities seemed indifferent. Finally a black farmer named Paul Bogle led a small uprising at Morant Bay, east of Kingston. The courthouse was burned and a few persons were killed. The island governor, Edward Eyre, took violent repressive measures, declaring martial law and sending out troops to capture anyone who looked dangerous. Bogle was taken and hanged. So was George Gordon, a mulatto landowner who knew Bogle but had no connection with the Morant Bay affair. In all, 439 people died at Eyre's order. Ultimately he was recalled, while Bogle and Gordon became national heroes.

This was virtually the only outbreak against authority in three centuries of English rule, with one exception that actually began earlier. When the Spaniards were forced to leave the island for Cuba, they freed most of their slaves. The latter joined others who had escaped to the hills and set up a kind of guerrilla state. The English called them Maroons, from the Spanish *cimarrón* (se-ma-RONE), meaning wild. They fought off the English for more than 80 years—three generations—until a truce was arranged.

By its terms, the Maroons received land in two mountainous areas "for themselves and posterity forever." The larger area is in the Cockpit Country, an almost impassable section of eroded limestone, thickly forested, with hundreds of big round depressions or "cockpits." It still is largely a blank on the map, though part of it is ominously marked District of Look Behind. Today some 8,000 Maroons proclaim their autonomy, though they do pay Jamaican taxes and vote in elections.

Officially, the island is governed from Kingston. In Spanish days the capital was about 13 miles west and called Villa de la Vega (VE-ya day la VAY-ga) or Town of the Plain. The English renamed it Spanish Town and kept it as their capital for two centuries. Around the old plaza they put up some of the finest red-brick, white-columned Georgian buildings in the hemisphere. Some of them still stand. But Spanish Town itself long ago was outstripped by Kingston, and in 1872 that became the capital.

Kingston spills down the lower slopes of green mountains to a beautiful blue harbor protected by the Palisadoes, a sandspit ten miles long. At the sandspit's tip is what is left of Port Royal, the "sin city" of pirate days until its destruction by earthquake in 1692. Various Port Royal relics—bottles, clay pipes, jewelry, coins, dishes, even building foundations—have been brought up from the harbor or revealed by excavation.

A city of low buildings, Kingston, Jamaica's present capital, fronts on a deep-water harbor where ships of many lands come and go. In the background are the Palisadoes and the open Caribbean Sea.

JAMAICA 83

Many tourists have seen Kingston's busy waterfront. Fewer know the Parade, where city buses start their runs in a great square that teems wtih humanity; the palm-shaded main campus of the University of the West Indies; the National Stadium; the downtown corner where six bookmakers operate almost side by side; the blocks of development housing; the modern shopping centers—or the slums.

The slums feed the anger of those who advocate "Black Power." Militant blacks say their people are victimized by whites, such as the bauxite extractors, and mulattoes, such as Jamaica's leaders. There is some historical background for this feeling.

When the mulattoes began moving into important positions on the island, many of them openly modeled themselves after the English. They drank tea, played cricket, dressed like Englishmen, read British books and newspapers, sent their children to British schools and universities. And they often looked down on former slaves of pure Negro blood.

At the same time, they wanted to be independent of their former masters. Mulattoes founded Jamaica's present major political parties, both dedicated to independence. One was Norman Manley, a lawyer educated at Oxford, who founded the People's National Party (PNP) in 1938. The other was Manley's cousin Alexander Bustamante, a labor leader of the 1930's who launched the Jamaica Labor Party (JLP) in 1944.

In 1958, with the PNP in power, Manley led Jamaica into the short-lived Federation of the West Indies. Britain had proposed this as a source of mutual support for ten of its colonies as they were granted independence. Manley believed that all ten needed one another. But Bustamante was opposed. He told the country that other islands could outvote Jamaica and would expect her, as the largest and richest, to pay all the bills. After three years the Jamaican legislature voted to withdraw from the Federation (which promptly collapsed), and the JLP rode to power when independence came in 1962.

Since then the two parties have taken turns running the country. They are not far apart in basic thinking, and the policies of one often are followed by the other. Black militants condemn them both.

84   HELLO, WEST INDIES

For the average Jamaican, politics are less immediate than the concerns of daily life: job, home and family, modest diversions. He makes small bets on football games and horse races. He relishes his meals, which are inclined to be spicy: pepperpot soup, thick chicken stew, mackerel with bananas, curried goat. (The so-called national dish is salt fish with ackee, a fruit originally from Africa that tastes something like eggs and something like chestnuts.) He likes movies, the radio, and television, but doesn't read a great deal beyond *The Daily Gleaner,* Jamaica's generally excellent newspaper.

Jamaica produces good writers, such as novelists John Hearne, Roger Mais, and Vic Reed, who are not widely popular but who speak, sometimes powerfully, for the developing self-awareness of their countrymen. There are poets, playwrights, and artists of repute. The work of all may be sampled in *Jamaica Journal,* a quarterly magazine published by the unusual Institute of Jamaica. This organization maintains a library on island matters that would do credit to a far larger country.

The average Jamaican looks forward to his free weekends. His wife, inclined to be more religious, looks forward to Sunday and church. About three-quarters of the population belong to Protestant congregations, some of them small and strictly local. A visitor noted one of the smallest in a one-room, one-story building on a Kingston side street. A large sign bravely proclaimed: "Church of God and Saints of Christ, Inc. Tabernacle #1."

Less formal faiths also flourish. Probably best known is *pukkumina,* a so-called revival cult that blends African and European forms of worship. There are various ceremonies, all with hymn-singing and Bible-reading led by a "shepherd" (usually a man). Most dramatic is the ritual for a specific purpose, such as a baptism or the giving of thanks. Typically this is held at night, indoors, with 50 or more worshipers (mostly women). The shepherd preaches, conducts hymns, and invokes the spirits. Musicians strike up on drums, tambourines, and maracas. The worshipers commence a rhythmic dance. Soon they start to inhale and exhale in repeated short gasps. Scientifically speaking, this reduces the amount of oxygen in the lungs and brings on dizziness. In *pukkumina* it may lead to unconsciousness, at which point the wor-

JAMAICA 85

shiper is said to be "possessed" by a spirit.* The ceremony goes on for hours or even days.

Except as a subject for dance theater, *pukkumina* rarely interests educated Jamaicans. Its main appeal is to the poor. The latter also are the strongest believers in folk tales and superstitions, of which the island has many. But even the sophisticated may be cautious about *duppies* or ghosts. You have to beware of duppies. Someone who knows how can "set" a duppy on you and cause all kinds of harm, though you may be able to fight back with another duppy. Sometimes you meet a duppy that has no immediate evil intent. The safest course is to cork it in a bottle and throw the bottle away. The duppy will stay there until someone breaks the bottle or pulls out the cork.

Jamaica has other supernatural creatures. One is the Rolling Calf, which has fiery eyes and drags a chain around in the night. The Three-Legged Horse may chase you if you are out too late. Then there is the Old Hige (or Hag), a woman who takes off her skin at night and wanders about, sometimes entering houses and sucking the blood of people asleep.

It all depends on what you want to believe in. Jamaica has one group of young to middle-aged men who vow that Emperor Haile Selassie of Ethiopia is God. Because he was named Ras Tafari before assuming the throne, they call themselves Ras Tafarians or "Rastas." They say they want to "return" to Ethiopia, one part of Africa from which no slaves ever were taken. They wear beards and long hair, smoke a lot of marijuana, and shout the motto "Peace and Love!" Asked what they will do when Haile Selassie dies, they simply laugh: since he is God he cannot die.

The idea of returning to Africa obsessed an earlier Jamaican to the point of really trying to make it possible. He was Marcus Garvey, born in 1887. As a young man he came to believe that Negroes in the New World would be better off if they could move to their ancestral homeland. He pushed his "Back to Africa" movement first in Britain, then in the United States. In 1919 he set up a steamship service called the Black Star Line which he

---

* Because of this feature, the cult often is called *pocomania,* a word wrongly believed to mean "little mania" in Spanish. Jamaican scholars prefer *pukkumina,* which apparently has an African root.

86 HELLO, WEST INDIES

planned to use in transporting Negroes to Africa. The American government objected to his fund-raising methods, and he wound up in jail. Freed in 1927, he returned to Jamaica. Finally he left for England and died there in 1940.

Garvey probably made more world headlines than any other Jamaican before or since. One of his biggest worries still is a major problem for his country: unemployment.

This shows much the same nature as on other islands. Basically, the farming economy cannot generate enough jobs to keep up with the population increase. And rural dwellers are turning away from the soil. They prefer almost anything else, but often can't find it. Normally about one worker in five is unemployed. The search for jobs is the major factor in creating Kingston's slums.

Equally urgent is the need for more and better schooling. In plantocracy days there were no schools for slave children, and relatively few were built in the century after emancipation. Free public education was available only through the sixth grade. That still is the rule in rural schools—and often the youngsters don't show up anyway. As one village teacher explains:

"I have a full class, or nearly so, just two days a week—Tuesday and Wednesday. On Thursday about half the children are out, helping Mama get ready for market day on Saturday. Friday, things must be carried to market and attendance is about ten percent. Saturday comes the market, Sunday everyone carries things home again, and Monday everyone rests up. Do you wonder that Jamaica has a high rate of illiteracy?"

Actually, the official rate is 15 percent—not bad for the West Indies—and schooling improves markedly in larger towns and cities. There, the biggest current need is for more secondary schools. And the curriculum is being overhauled. "We've imitated the British too long," an official comments. "We need more studies specifically planned for Jamaica."

He cites an example: "We've begun a required course in agriculture for both boys and girls. It runs three years, grades seven through nine. It covers all the basic things a Jamaican farmer needs—soil types, animal husbandry, crop management, and so on. Each school will have its own five-acre farm for the students'

Powerful machines scrape up and carry off the red earth that yields Jamaica's main export, bauxite, for processing into aluminum. When mining is finished, the surface will be smoothed and replanted.

use. And here's our special feature: the manager of each farm will be expected to make it pay.

"Why? No, not just to save money. We want to convince these youngsters that farming is a good way of life—and at least as profitable as doing odd jobs in Montego Bay."

The schools already have produced able performers in the field of sports. Among many track-and-field stars, runner Herb McKenley stands out with five medals in the 1948 and 1952 Olympics. A younger speedster, Don Quarrie, set a world indoor record of 9.3 seconds for the 100-yard dash in 1971. Other champions have appeared in such diverse fields as boxing, shooting, and water polo. Jamaican cricketers join those from Barbados and Trinidad in the West Indies teams that play international matches against Great Britain, Australia, New Zealand, India, and Pakistan.

88   HELLO, WEST INDIES

Helped by bauxite and tourism, Jamaica today is encouraging new industries even as it trains workers for them. The future is not all bleak. But there are contrasts on the island to make one wonder. A showplace of the northeast coast is Frenchman's Cove, probably the most expensive hotel on earth, where (as this is written) the rate is $240 a day for two in the desirable winter season. In two days, a visiting couple spends more than the average Jamaican's *yearly* income.

The Cayman Islands

Three pretty little islands, the Caymans (KAY-mans), lie spaced well apart in an east-west line starting about 130 miles northwest of Jamaica's western tip. Formerly a Jamaican dependency, they now are a British colony of only 93 square miles and about 9,000 people. The latter catch sharks, turtles, and sponges, and go to sea to send money home. Lately tourists have discovered the Caymans' beaches, fishing, and quiet charm, and the fact that on Grand Cayman, the main island of the three, is a perfectly proper little village named Hell.

10

HAITI

It is night in Haiti. In a thatched hut on the outskirts of Port-au-Prince, the capital, a black priestess sifts cornmeal through her fingers onto the dirt floor. Swiftly it forms a complicated pattern, made up in part of the symbols of ancient African nature gods called *loas* (pronounced lwas). These include wise old Legba, most powerful of them all; Erzulie, goddess of love; Damballa, her favorite husband; Ogoun, god of warfare. Tonight the gods are being invoked from their homes far across the ocean. . . .

Drummers grip wooden tom-toms between bare knees, beating out steady rhythms with tireless fingers. They have been drumming for hours; they will keep on for hours. In the small, confined hut the thudding brings a kind of intoxication.

Now a shuffling dance begins, bare feet scattering the cornmeal. The priest offers prayers to Legba, to Erzulie, to other *loas*. The drumbeat quickens. Flickering lamplight shows black bodies dancing ever faster, faces eager with anticipation. Will the *loas* come soon?

The priest and his helpers offer sacrifices to the gods. Two roosters are killed, then a male goat. The blood is caught in sacred vessels. The air in the hut has grown thick, almost unbreathable. Surely the *loas* are coming now?

It happens. Amid the frenzied movement, a young woman stops, reels backward, and falls. Her face is contorted. Her eyes are shut. She is panting, sweating, clawing at her clothes. The priestess holds her hands. Then like a sleepwalker the woman rises, eyes blank, and begins a private dance. Her step is mincing and coquettish. She smiles seductively.

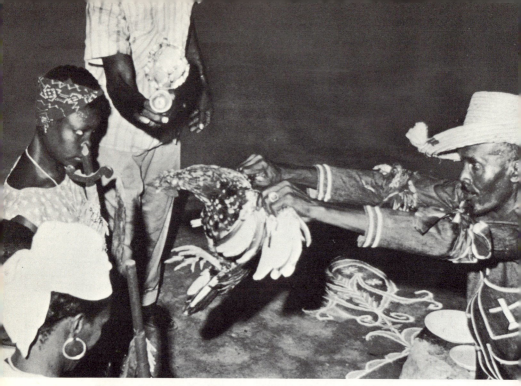

Before fascinated believers, a live rooster becomes a sacrifice to the loas *in a voodoo ceremony. The design on the floor, a flour* vever, *shortly will be erased by the feet of shuffling worshipers.*

"Erzulie has come to her," an onlooker whispers. "Now she will win the love of the one she wants."

Soon other worshipers are visited by other *loas*. Each staggers and falls, gasping, then stands again to act according to the nature of "his" *loa*. Warlike Ogoun fights furiously against invisible enemies. Old Legba limps painfully, and someone hands him a cane. The drums beat faster and louder, sweat pours and smoke thickens, the dark hut seems alive with spirit presences that will fly back to Africa only after hours or days, when their work here is finished. . . .

Such in bare outline is a typical ceremony in the great cult of voodoo, native to Haiti and devoutly followed by probably the majority of the blacks who form 95 percent of the people. The rest, mulattoes of relatively high class and light skin, scorn voodoo. The Catholic Church, which claims nine out of ten Haitians as members, condemns voodoo. But for the mass of people voodoo is a living faith, a source of comfort, and an answer to problems.

Voodoo belief includes a remote supreme god, the Great Mas-

HAITI 91

ter, who judges men but has no direct contact with them. That is made by the scores of *loas*, whom the Great Master authorizes to dispense both good and evil. Voodoo ceremonies are designed to win favorable attention from *loas*. Worshipers seek their aid for many reasons, from strictly material (for example, to be cured of an illness) to spiritual or even superstitious (for example, to appease the angry soul of a dead person). Success is promised when a *loa* enters or "possesses" the worshiper.

What is "possession"? Students of voodoo generally call it a form of self-hypnosis that starts in childhood. The average Haitian grows up believing completely in *loas*. When he seeks their help, he also seeks to be "possessed." The voodoo ceremony works him up to an emotional peak. Finally he can take no more and falls unconscious. Thereafter, so long as the seizure lasts, he acts as one "possessed" *should* act.

The persistence of voodoo through several centuries says a lot about the people of Haiti. It is a religion for the poor and downtrodden. For Haitians.

Their poverty is deep, long standing, and getting worse. Five million of them live jammed into the western third of the island of Hispaniola, a mountainous area little larger than Vermont. Descendants of slaves brought in by French planters, they inhabit the second oldest republic in the hemisphere (proclaimed January 1, 1804) and the only one where French is the official language (although almost everyone speaks a patois called Créole). They won freedom through violent revolution, but they never built a stable society or a sound economy.

Today most Haitians are small farmers, living in dirt-floored shacks and taking a bare living from the increasingly eroded soil. The average farm is about big enough for one family, but steady population growth makes the average farm ever smaller. Schooling is poor in the cities, almost nonexistent elsewhere: perhaps one Haitian in five can read and write. Medical care is so sketchy that average life expectancy is 40 years, compared to, say, 65 in nearby Jamaica. Like a poor relation, Haiti gets help from the United Nations, the Organization of American States, various governments, even foundations. But the help only puts off problems. It cannot solve them.

92   HELLO, WEST INDIES

One more statistic sums it up: the average income in Haiti is $80 a year. Among other things, this explains why there are more beggars on Haiti than the rest of the Antilles put together.

Yet neither poverty nor despair has soured the Haitian people. Most of them remain somehow gentle, cordial, and good humored. Their songs and dances break out not just in voodoo rituals but in many everyday experiences. Folk songs, work songs, party songs (as for Carnival), and others run to the hundreds. Many observers have remarked that Haitians seem to have an indestructible vitality. They live with adversity, yet they can laugh about it.

On the map Haiti is shaped something like the open mouth of a fantastic animal, facing west. The upper jaw points toward Cuba, 50 miles away; the lower, toward Jamaica. Between them is the wide Gulf of Gonave (Go-NAHV), sheltering the 40-mile-long island of the same name. At the gulf's inner end stands Port-au-Prince, chief Haitian port and metropolis, with about a quarter million residents. Lesser ports are on the north, gulf, and south coasts. All are most easily reached from the capital by air, since Haiti has just one good road. It runs up the mountains behind Port-au-Prince to the suburb of Pétionville (1,500 feet) and the resort of Kenscoff (5,000 feet)—a total distance of 17 miles.

"Beyond the mountains," says a Haitian proverb, "are more mountains." They rise to above 8,000 feet near the eastern border with the Dominican Republic. Their choppiness helps make Haiti's rainfall very spotty—here torrential, there nil. Small valleys and hilly slopes are a patchwork of farms growing coffee and food crops. Lower flatlands may yield sugar, cacao, cotton, and sisal (used in ropemaking). A little bauxite and copper is exported. There is almost no industry.

Most consumer goods come from the United States, Japan, or France, but few people can afford the costlier items. They just "make do." Everything from cars and appliances to cans and clothespins is used until it refuses to function. Visitors to Port-au-Prince often marvel that the battered old taxis run at all. There are few private autos or motorcycles, many bicycles and horse-drawn vehicles. People ride bony donkeys along the main streets.

HAITI 93

There also are airless little buses with doors at the back, jauntily painted and sporting names like "My Secret Love" or "God Is with Me."

Most streets in the capital are tree lined but dirty, with pavement often broken or blocked by excavations. Sidewalks may be even more hazardous. Most buildings are low and iron roofed, many painted white but in poor repair. One section of wooden houses in gingerbread style, all cupolas, balconies, and fretwork, reveals the taste of the mulatto *élite* who had them built in the early 1900's. Later the owners moved to more modern homes up in Pétionville, which has cooler air and a better view.

Port-au-Prince has hundreds of small neighborhood stores, some big public markets, and a downtown area that might be labeled smart in a less rickety capital. And there is one stretch of several blocks along one side of one street that must be unique. In it are more than 40 stores, almost all of one room, all selling one thing: cheap shoes.

Larger capital structures are mainly government buildings or churches. A gambling casino stands on the waterfront boulevard named Président Truman. Not far off is the stadium where soccer and other games are played, often under floodlights to foil the hot sun. But the biggest thing in town is Independence Heroes Square, a parklike area with wide paved walkways, statues of historic Haitian figures, trees, lawns, benches, and fountains. People stroll through to savor the contrast with the rest of the city. Young men pace back and forth, apparently talking to themselves—students memorizing poetry. On the square is the National Palace, where Haiti's presidents live. It is glaringly white by day, spotlighted at night, and constantly guarded by soldiers.

Some visitors miss the square because they are busy visiting art galleries. Poverty or no, Haiti is the only Antillean country that has produced a major art movement. It has surprised and impressed people all over the world, including Haitians.

It came about because an American artist named DeWitt Peters, touring Haiti, noted some brightly painted frescoes of birds, fruit, and flowers on the doors of a village bar. Curious, he learned they had been done by a self-taught artist—and voodoo priest—named Hector Hippolyte (E-po-LEET). Peters

This rural Haitian town typifies much of the country. The houses are small, unpainted, roofed with iron. The streets are little more than dusty paths. But trees, shrubs, and vines grow luxuriantly.

looked further and found so many more signs of unrecognized talent that in 1944 he opened the Art Center in Port-au-Prince to display and sell Haitian works. Within a few years the newborn Haitian "school" was being exhibited widely in America and Europe.

Good Haitian paintings (also wood carvings and sculpture) show vitality, originality, and an intense feel for color. Some painters pick realistic subjects—a village street, a barnyard, a slave market. Others paint the fantastic—voodoo *loas* and Catholic saints, devils and wizards, ghosts, dead men. Hector Hippolyte painted not only voodoo subjects but the reverse side of the cult, Wanga or black magic. (This corresponds to *obeah*. In Haiti, a voodoo priest also may function as a Wanga priest, calling up "underworld" *loas*—the opposite of those normally sought —to work evil.) Some artists have produced deeply religious works. Two outstanding names here are Philomé Obin (O-

BANH) and Wilson Bigaud (Be-GO). Both contributed to some remarkable murals which, because the Catholic Church was against so-called popular art, were placed in the Episcopal Cathedral of Port-au-Prince.

Hippolyte, Obin, and Bigaud showed the way for dozens of younger Haitians. Most have been self-taught and paint as they "feel." Much Haitian art has proved to be a good investment. One Port-au-Prince dealer recently offered any painting in his stock with a guarantee that the buyer could return it after a year if he didn't like it and get his money back plus 12 percent.

Local paintings are for sale in just about every hotel, most of which are surprisingly comfortable, with outstanding food. Tucked in odd corners of Port-au-Prince and Pétionville, they date largely from the 1950's, when Haiti attracted many tourists. Today visitors are fewer. Some are repelled by the rundown condition of the country, the beggars, the bad roads, the language

Mammoth monument to pride and fear, Henri Christophe's Citadelle Laferrière bulks against the dry hills of northern Haiti. It has no neighbors, and no tenants—except possibly Christophe's ghost.

96   HELLO, WEST INDIES

barrier. And some frankly fear violence—for Haiti has a long record of dictatorship and brutality.

Its roots lie deep in the excesses of slavery. In Caribbean terms, this began late. Although Hispaniola was the Spaniards' first colony (the Arawaks called the whole island Haiti, "Land of Mountains"), they focused on the eastern end, Santo Domingo. Later they drove the Brethren of the Coast off Tortuga, near the northwest coast, but hardly noticed when some Frenchmen quietly moved across to Haiti. There the newcomers soon were reinforced from France. Planting began and towns were laid out, including Cap Haïtien on the north coast, which still has pastel-colored houses with balconies and red roofs from those days. War was raging in Europe (as usual), and Spain made little objection when a 1697 treaty gave France the western part of Hispaniola.

The new owners of Saint-Domingue (Santo Domingo in French) moved fast. The Haitian lowlands were quilted with sugar, cacao, and other plantations. By the middle of the eighteenth century Saint-Domingue ranked as the richest colonial possession on earth. In that century an estimated one million slaves were imported to work the fields and staff the planters' mansions.

Treated little better than domestic animals, the slaves nurtured a deep hatred for their masters. When the French Revolution broke out in 1789, a few mulattoes sought rights for their people. They were cruelly executed. Then in 1791 three black leaders (one a voodoo priest) met near Cap Haïtien and took a blood oath that whites must be exterminated. A week later the slaves in the north burst forth like lava from a volcano. They massacred landowners and their families, burned houses and crops, and stopped only when there was nothing more to destroy.

The French authorities retaliated with equal ferocity, and open warfare raged for several years. Even after slavery was declared at an end, the bloodletting went on. English troops seized this moment to invade Haiti, and in 1795 Spain ceded all of the island to France. Out of the turmoil appeared a former slave, Toussaint l'Ouverture (Too-SANH loo-vair-TEUR), leading a makeshift army that ousted not only the English but the French also. He then set up his own government and in 1801 proclaimed himself governor for life.

HAITI   97

Back in France, Napoleon Bonaparte took this as black effrontery. He ordered his wife's brother, General Charles Leclerc, to gather the largest force yet to cross the Atlantic (an estimated 40,000 men) and punish Toussaint. The force retook most of Hispaniola, reestablished slavery, persuaded Toussaint to lay down his arms, then trapped him by a ruse and took him to France, where he died in prison.

Toussaint's generals now led a bloody new uprising. Helped by yellow fever, which killed thousands of French soldiers (and Leclerc himself), they forced a final French withdrawal. Surviving planters and their families fled. Jean Jacques Dessalines (Des-sa-LEEN) proclaimed independence and was crowned Emperor Jacques I of Haiti, restoring the old Indian name. He also created the Haitian flag from the red, white, and blue French tricolor: he tore out the white stripe.

Dessalines ruled only two years, being assassinated by his own palace guard. Haiti then split in two, each section under a general.

Henri Christophe (Cre-STOFF) set himself up in the north. He was a huge black who, with some 800 other Haitians, had fought in the American Revolution. Now, calling himself Emperor Henri I, he established his court at Cap Haïtien. He created his own nobility and organized an efficient government based on discipline. People who worked, prospered. But Henri was carried away by self-esteem. He built nine different palaces, including world-renowned Sans Souci in a valley south of Cap Haïtien. This classic building, the match of virtually any palace in Europe, is four stories high and is situated on 20 acres. On completion in 1813 it had interior walls of mahogany, floors of marble, imported furniture and draperies. Its sweeping entrance staircases and brick walls still are there.

But the almost incredible monument to this illiterate former slave is the Citadelle Laferrière (named for one of its architects) on a secluded mountain 3,000 feet high and two hours by horseback from Sans Souci. The visitor must ride in because the only road is a trail. Henri wanted it so. He conceived the citadel as a refuge if Napoleon tried again to take Haiti, and it resembles a fortress of the Middle Ages, with walls 12 feet thick at the base

98   HELLO, WEST INDIES

and 140 feet tall. Conscript labor carried in all the building materials and wrestled 365 heavy bronze cannon into place. The ten years of construction reportedly required 200,000 men and killed 20,000 of them. Visitors may explore many of the citadel's scores of rooms, from dungeons to bedrooms. Others remain sealed to this day.

Compared with Henri Christophe, his rival in southern Haiti was mild and undramatic. He was Alexandre Pétion (PAY-tyoNg), a mulatto educated in France. Ruling in Port-au-Prince, he broke up former plantations into small plots and gave them to former slaves. He did not realize that eventually this practice would make most Haitians land-starved peasants.

Henri Christophe gradually lost popular support until finally even his soldiers deserted him. Half paralyzed by a stroke, he shot himself. His tomb stands in his awesome Citadelle.

Pétion died about the same time, though peacefully. He was succeeded by Jean Pierre Boyer (BWA-yay), who reunited Haiti and proclaimed the whole island, including Santo Domingo, a republic. France recognized the nation in 1838. But Boyer was forced out five years later, Santo Domingo broke away for good, and Haiti never regained the glamor and glory of the early years.

Instead, the country fell prey to a parade of dictators who, though partly or wholly black, looked on their countrymen mainly as objects to be exploited. In 1849, President Faustin Soulouque (Soo-LUKE) named himself Emperor Faustin I; he lived up to the title for nine years, when a revolution threw him out. Other presidents came and went, generally looting the national treasury in passing. By 1915 conditions were so chaotic that a particularly unpopular president was literally torn apart by an outraged mob. The United States then sent Marines to restore order and established a protectorate over Haiti. It lasted until 1934.

Representative works by largely self-taught Haitian painters are displayed in Port-au-Prince. Their subject matter reflects the artists' daily contacts with animals, flowers, birds—and people.

100 HELLO, WEST INDIES

Foreign occupation for nearly a generation seems to have spurred nationalistic feelings in Haiti. The 1920's produced several prominent writers, of whom the best known abroad are Jacques Romain and the Marcelin brothers, Pierre and Philippe-Thoby. In music, Justin Elie won fame as a composer. Later came the outstanding dancer Jean Justiné, and then the Haitian painting explosion.

After the Americans withdrew, politics went on as usual. In 1937 there was an ugly international incident. Uncounted Haitians had crossed the border into the Dominican Republic and begun farming on land not legally theirs. The Dominicans naturally were angry. Finally their notorious dictator, Rafael Trujillo (Troo-HE-yo), sent troops to clear out the squatters. In doing so, they massacred an estimated 15,000 Haitians in cold blood.

A few years later Haiti produced a dictator of equal caliber. He was François Duvalier (Du-VAL-yay), a doctor educated partly in the United States. He got into politics by leading underground resistance to the oppressive President Paul Magloire (Ma-GLWAHR). The latter resigned in 1956 and Duvalier was chosen to succeed him. Duvalier said he would help the black Haitians, long victimized by the mulatto *élite*. Events soon proved otherwise.

Papa Doc, as he wanted to be called, took a firm grip on the government. He had himself named President for Life and Renovator of the Nation. He then set about renovating his own fortune. Though his presidential salary was $14,000 a year, he soon owned property and businesses valued in the millions, with more millions safely hidden in Swiss banks. His methods included the collection of illegal taxes, forced "contributions" from the well off (with smaller amounts from average citizens), and outright bribery. To enforce his wishes, Duvalier recruited a special militia known as the *Tonton Macoute*—Créole for bogeymen—whose members were empowered to shoot first and talk later.

Like Fidel Castro in Cuba, Duvalier exiled many educated and well-to-do persons who opposed him. Some similarly tried to fight back via invasion. Most attempts were almost ludicrous— a raid by a single small plane dropping small bombs that missed, vain attempts to shell the Palace from ancient warships in the

HAITI 101

harbor. After each attack Papa Doc methodically executed persons who might have had something to do with it: army or navy officers, relatives of the raiders, and so on. Haitians got the message.

In 1971, after years of failing health, Duvalier died. His chosen successor was his nineteen-year-old son, Jean Claude. (The Haitian constitution had made forty the minumum age for a president, so Papa Doc changed the constitution.) Whether or not the boy stayed in power, few Haitians expected many other changes. For most, the prospect was poverty and oppression as usual.

11

THE DOMINICAN REPUBLIC

The eastern two thirds of Hispaniola is occupied by the Dominican Republic. Though only a winding line on the map separates it from Haiti (Hispaniola here is about 110 miles wide), the two countries differ in many ways.

With 19,129 square miles and about four million people, the Dominican Republic is twice as big as Haiti and much less crowded. Its people are only 15 percent black, with another 15 percent white and the rest mulatto. Dominicans speak neither French nor Créole, but Spanish; they play soccer but vastly prefer baseball; they show scant interest in voodoo; they have at least some industry (food processing, cement, textiles); their income per person is nearly four times that in Haiti. And they celebrate winning their independence not from a European power but from Haiti itself.

Haiti occupied Santo Domingo (as it then was called) from 1821 to 1844, and Dominicans have not forgotten. Their distaste for their neighbors takes odd forms. Many young women regularly wear hair curlers in public; they want to straighten any kinkiness that might appear Negroid. The late Dictator Trujillo, a mulatto, tried to assure foreigners that he was white. Such things are not anti-Negro (there is virtually no discrimination within the Dominican Republic) but anti-Haitian. While thousands of Haitians cross the border to work on Dominican farms, few Dominicans visit Haiti for any reason.

Nevertheless, Dominicans have at least one reason to thank poor, much abused Haiti: it makes their country look good by comparison. For the Dominican Republic is itself poor and

THE DOMINICAN REPUBLIC 103

abused. If its income per person outstrips Haiti's, the figure still is lower than in any other independent Antillean country. Dominican life expectancy is only 50 years. And about one Dominican in three cannot read or write.

The country has some notable natural gifts. The central Cibao Valley is one of the most fertile areas anywhere, with topsoil up to several feet deep; it grows mainly sugar, cacao, and coffee. Nearby mountains contain almost untouched deposits of iron ore, bauxite, nickel, and other minerals. There are many things to attract tourists—sun, sand, sea, greenery, hotels, history, highways. At one time Americans were so attracted that our government actually expected to buy the whole country for $150,000. Congress disapproved and the deal fell through. That was in 1869. Today, few Americans seem to want any part of the Dominican Republic, even as a gift.

The main reason is the same one that haunts many other small nations: political instability. The Dominican Republic has been independent well over a century, but its history is one of almost continual upheaval, with civil war, dictatorship, and assassination a recurring cycle. In its first 122 years the country had a staggering total of 71 presidents. Not surprisingly, a favorite game of Dominican boys is "war," with wooden guns carefully whittled to look like the real thing.

The Republic's present low estate is in marked contrast with its importance four centuries and more ago. Its city of Santo Domingo was Spain's first colonial capital and colonizing center. It was compactly set against the west bank of the Ozama River, protected by a wall with well-guarded gates. Within the wall arose the New World's first chapel, cathedral, monastery, hospital, and university. (At least some part of all of them still stands.) Through the streets moved soldiers and merchants, Madrid-appointed officials and churchmen, enslaved Indians and Africans. The harbor throbbed with shipping.

All this traces to the accident of history that made Hispaniola the first island ·colonized by Columbus. He and his family figure in much of its early history. In 1496, on his second voyage, Columbus left his brother Bartolomé in charge of a settlement on the north coast. Bartolomé moved to Santo Domingo's present

104   HELLO, WEST INDIES

location because it had a good harbor, good land—and gold. Its name is another accident: he founded it on August 4, which happens to be the feast day of Bartolomé's favorite saint, Santo Domingo de Guzmán.

When the colonists grew restless and Madrid sent out Governor Bobadilla, both brothers went to Spain as prisoners. Both soon were freed, but neither got back to Santo Domingo. The island nonetheless is advertised today as "the land Columbus loved." Perhaps he did. In any case, his son Diego, who had married a niece of Spain's King Fernando, was named viceroy and governor general in 1509, and settled down to stay. Nineteen years later, his son Luis, the Admiral's grandson, became the first student enrolled at the University of St. Thomas Aquinas, direct ancestor of today's University of Santo Domingo.

Diego Columbus built a palace beside the Ozama that dazzled Spanish America. Men came there to discuss big plans, to enjoy the elegance and culture of the court, to ask favors or conduct intrigues. None of this was destined to endure. As Santo Domingo's gold ran out, the conquistadors shifted their sights westward. Diego died. The palace was abandoned, and in 1586 it was sacked, with the rest of the city, by Sir Francis Drake. Eventually, hardly an original stone remained. But today the whole building has been reconstructed and filled with Spanish antiques. It makes a high point in a tour of the city.

The same can be said of the cathedral, begun in 1514. This contains a unique treasure: the bones of Christopher Columbus, brought from Spain in 1544. The Spanish government donated a huge, ornate bronze-and-marble tomb for them in 1892, as a 400th-anniversary memento. Placed just inside the cathedral entrance, it nearly touches the vaulted roof and makes worshipers detour around it.

All the capital's ancient structures are inside the original wall in what has become the downtown area. Along the narrow streets are buildings basically colonial in style—flush to the sidewalk, rarely more than three stories high, many with balconies where people can sit and watch the traffic. Street floors are occupied largely by stores, banks, and offices. Sidewalk venders offer bags and belts of goatskin, dolls from Hong Kong, big red American

THE DOMINICAN REPUBLIC 105

apples, live chickens, and jewelry of amber, a Dominican specialty. Passersby add color: a barefoot boy in rags; a gentleman in white suit, white shoes, and white straw hat; a typical young man in sandals, dark slacks, and pink shirt worn outside; his better-off friend with shirt tucked in, dark tie, and jacket; women in everything from the country girl's sandals, skirt, and blouse to the latest style and hairdo from the United States. At noon, practically the whole area shuts down so people can go home for lunch and a nap.

The old wall is gone, except for two weatherbeaten gates. Santo Domingo has grown far beyond them, with a population now above 600,000. Westward stretch wider streets faced with houses, some little more than shacks, some large and comfortable, some compactly modern. There are hotels and fairly elegant restaurants. In the latter, men ordinarily dine with other men, an old Spanish custom. This section includes housing developments, a zoo, a drive-in movie, two universities, and several streets named for American presidents. There also are two short streets bafflingly called Boy Scouts and Cub Scouts (in English).

Outside the capital, relatively good roads run the length and width of the country. One leads northwest to Santiago in the Cibao Valley. This is the second city of the Republic, but far smaller and less sophisticated than Santo Domingo. Horse-drawn buggies vie with taxis in the squeezed-in streets, landowning families boast of their *criollo* (not Spanish) forebears, and girls are chaperoned into their twenties. Santiago has the country's third university, and a small restaurant serving at last count 16 flavors of home-made ice cream, including chocolate almond, pineapple, and tamarind.

Country villages are something else. Typically, a village straggles for a mile or more along a main road, with virtually no cross streets. Many residents normally go barefoot, and men often spend the day shirtless. Houses crowd close to the road. Small, built of the simplest materials, usually dirt floored, the houses are used mainly for sleeping. Cooking normally is done over an outdoor fire, and one iron pot holds the family dinner of rice and beans or *sancocho* (a meat-and-vegetable stew regarded as the national dish).

Seated three to a bench and not all wearing shoes, these Dominican children are getting as much education as their country is able to give them. Better schooling is coming, but slowly and expensively.

Different still is Sosúa, a unique community on the north coast. Here, at government invitation, some 600 Jewish refugees from Europe settled during World War II. (No other country made such an offer.) Starting modestly as farmers, they gradually got into cheese making and today produce about a quarter of the country's supply. A separate plant packs sausages. With the years, many of the original group have died or moved away, but the survivors have prospered and reared children who are true Dominicans.

Schools in the Dominican Republic do a fair job up to sixth grade, a poor one from then on. (Only about two students in one hundred finish high school.) Courses are similar to those in other

THE DOMINICAN REPUBLIC 107

West Indian lands, but this is the only country with two separate school calendars for rural children in primary grades. The reason is that coffee is a major crop for many *campesinos*. When the berries ripen in the fall, the farmers cannot afford paid labor to pick them but depend on a concerted family effort. So, while about five out of six children attend school from October through June, the rest attend from January through September and spend most of their "summer vacation" harvesting coffee.

School sports are none too well organized, but almost every boy grows up playing baseball. There is a four-team professional league, and the country has sent many players to the United States, including such noted big-leaguers as Juan Marichal, Rico Carty, and the three Alou brothers. Other popular sports are softball, basketball, and volleyball. In 1968, lightweight Carlos Cruz became the first Dominican to win a world professional boxing championship. Tragically, he was killed the next year in an airplane crash.

Some Dominicans may have said Cruz died because a spell had been put on him—for Dominicans tend to be superstitious. Most are Catholics, but many go to spiritists or "witch doctors" for help in times of trouble. Some peasants believe in the existence of such forest creatures as the *ciguapa* (se-GWA-pa), which has a human body with the feet on backwards. Even the educated may feel it is bad luck to kill a pigeon, or to hand someone a salt cellar at the table. (Set it near him and let him pick it up himself.)

Few Dominicans have distinguished themselves culturally, in part because their land so long has been in turmoil. Recent years have brought recognition to painters Jaime Colson and Darío Suro. In a somewhat related field, Oscar de la Renta is a well-known dress designer. And the popular dance called the merengue (meh-REN-gay) was born in the Republic—unless, as some think, it actually began in Haiti as the *meringue* (meh-RANG).

Today's Dominican shows few traces of Indian blood, but the Indian past lingers. People still call the country Quisqueya (Kees-KAY-ya), the original Arawak name, and admire a brave chief named Guarocuya (Wa-ro-COO-ya). Reared by monks and christened Enriqué (En-REE-kay) or Henry, he was nicknamed

108   HELLO, WEST INDIES

Enriquillo—"Hank." He grew up to lead some of his people into the mountains and fight off Spanish attacks so successfully that Emperor Charles V finally let the group live (and die) in peace. Enriquillo is a national hero. A salty lake in the dry southwest, about 25 miles long and 144 feet below sea level, is named for him; it is the largest lake in the country, and in the West Indies. *Enriquillo* also is a book by Dominican Manuel Galván, written in 1882 but still considered an important Caribbean novel.

Once the Spaniards focused their attention on the mainland, Hispaniola practically fell asleep. In 1655 there was a brief flurry when an English force tried to capture Santo Domingo but was beaten off. (It went on to take Jamaica.) Cession of Haiti to France in 1697 caused little excitement. But the French Revolution and the Haitian slave outbreaks finally woke up the Dominicans.

Educated young *criollos* began plotting independence from Spain. Their hopes faltered when Spain rather abruptly handed all Hispaniola to France. Then the ferocious Haitians broke the French grip on their end of the island, and in 1809 the Dominicans did likewise. In 1814 another European treaty gave Santo Domingo back to Spain. Seven years later the Dominicans rewon their freedom—Spain was too busy elsewhere to pay much attention—only to lose it again to Haiti.

Foreign domination lasted 22 years. It ended suddenly when a secret patriotic society seized a number of Haitian garrisons and raised the Dominican flag. Three men led the revolt: Juan Pablo Duarte, Francisco Sánchez, and Ramon Mella (MAY-ya). All now are enshrined as heroes. Their remains lie under a gate in the old city wall, an eternal flame burns outside, and an honor guard stands watch.

Sad to say, the three had little chance to enjoy their triumph. They favored a completely independent Dominican Republic, but two top army generals said the little country needed outside help. One general, Pedro Santana, was the country's first elected president. Backed by the other, Buenaventura Báez (BA-ess), he sent Duarte, Sánchez, and Mella into exile.

The generals then fell out. Báez exiled Santana and offered the country to, in order, the United States, France, and Spain. His efforts were interrupted when Santana came back and started a civil

THE DOMINICAN REPUBLIC 109

war. The fighting wrecked homes and property, and American residents were in danger of starvation until a warship arrived with food. On request, the ship's commander mediated between Santana and Báez. The result was to return Santana to the presidency, where he soon succeeded where Báez had failed: he gave the country to Spain.

If all this sounds comical, it surely was not so for the Dominicans. In 1863, after two years of renewed colonial rule, they once more revolted and restored the republic, such as it was. Still lacking almost everything a going nation needs, it suffered one unscrupulous leader after another. Debts piled up, unrest became chronic, and in 1916 the United States Marines arrived to enforce order. They landed a year after those in Haiti and got out ten years sooner, in 1924.

Dominicans did not enjoy independence long. In 1930 the country was taken over by one of the foulest dictators this century has produced, Rafael Leonidas Trujillo.

Books have been written about the colossal ego and cynical cruelty of Trujillo, and the way he turned the Dominican Republic into a private estate. He seized power as a young lieutenant by plotting a military coup and, when it succeeded, liquidating his fellow plotters. Thereafter he built up a personal army, a vicious secret police, a nationwide spy system, a controlled press—all to insure that he could control the nation's sources of wealth, from ownership of most of the paying businesses to grinding taxation of the rest. His personal fortune eventually was estimated at $150,-000,000. Lesser fortunes were showered on his numerous family, his henchmen, and his friends.

Trujillo could indulge any whim, and did. He commissioned his eldest son an army colonel at the age of four. He changed the centuries-old name of Santo Domingo to Ciudad Trujillo, or Trujillo City. He had a mansion built just for lavish parties, and flew guests in from New York. To help keep the capital quiet, he ordered all pushcart venders to rubber-tire their carts. He spent millions on an "international fair" to show off his clean, well-run, progressive nation. Half a million visitors were expected; 24,000 showed up.

The man even did evil at a distance. When Venezuelan Presi-

110 HELLO, WEST INDIES

dent Rómulo Betancourt inveighed against him, Trujillo tried to have Betancourt killed. When a Spanish refugee wrote a book criticizing him, Trujillo had the writer kidnaped from New York, taken to Santo Domingo, and executed.

Trujillo's power finally was broken by the enemies he created. On a spring evening in 1961, two carloads of them intercepted his limousine and shot him down. Most people greeted the news with wild enthusiasm. Some former Trujillo favorites hastily sent their money out of the country, or fled themselves, but others stayed to try to hang on to businesses the dictator had helped make prosperous. Then the army got control of the situation and things grew less tense.

Since Trujillo's death, the Dominican Republic has tried to achieve stability and start moving forward. It has been difficult indeed. Thirty-one years of dictatorship, capping all the country's earlier troubles, have left deep divisions and bitterly opposed people.

In 1962 an election was held. Juan Bosch, a tall, blue-eyed professor who promised social progress, became president. The progress did not follow. In a few months the army removed Bosch and set a three-man civilian group in his place. Bosch left the country for Puerto Rico. His leftist supporters then recruited some military men and overthrew the ruling threesome. Regular army units fought back, but at first it seemed that the rebels would win.

From Washington, D.C., the situation looked like another Cuba. Hastily troops were sent to the Dominican Republic to try to keep the battling groups separated. They were only partly successful. Some Dominicans (and Americans) believe our troops saved the country from communism. Others say we only helped the rightists —the army and the rich. In any case, fighting lasted until the Organization of American States stepped in, merged the American troops into a peace-keeping force with small units from five Latin

A statue of Rafael Trujillo receives rough treatment after the dictator's assassination in 1961. Trujillo had monuments to himself placed all over the country. Today, even his name is hard to find.

112 HELLO, WEST INDIES

American countries, and arranged a cease-fire. The last foreign soldiers left in 1966.

Another election was held, with Bosch back as a candidate. He was opposed by short, bespectacled Joaquín Balaguer (Wha-KEEN Ba-la-GAIR), a bachelor lawyer and onetime Trujillo supporter. He campaigned vigorously and won. Bosch left for Spain, but hard feelings remained. "If hatred were edible," Balaguer said on taking office, "the Dominicans would easily be the best-fed people in the world."

Balaguer's prescription for the country was a stable government that would attract foreign investors. Helped by massive American aid, he improved the status of agriculture and local business, meanwhile putting some money into education and housing. But he did little about such basic problems as land distribution to poor *campesinos,* and unemployment actually increased under his administration. The search for jobs led many Dominicans to the United States, legally or not.* Critics of Balaguer's administration were taken in hand by police or the army. When he had the law changed so he could run for a second term in 1970, it seemed that a new version of Trujillo might be in the making.

The election itself passed peacefully. Many voters abstained, and Balaguer won again. With military and industrial support, he appeared set to follow his own course indefinitely. But opposition, open or hidden, continued. "The longer we postpone taking the lid off," one citizen observed, "the greater will be the explosion."

---

* Thousands may have come as tourists, then stayed on illegally by posing as Puerto Ricans or Cubans. Many other tricks are tried. For example, 23 Dominicans flew to Puerto Rico and claimed to be members of a championship softball team there by invitation. They might have gotten away with it if airport authorities had not noted that the "team" carried no equipment. All 23 were sent home.

12

PUERTO RICO

What is Puerto Rico? Various answers are possible, but none of them really is complete.

Puerto Rico is a beautiful tropical island, smallest of the Greater Antilles, a near rectangle 100 miles long and 35 miles wide. It lies 60 miles east of Hispaniola, 885 miles southeast of Florida, and about three hours from New York by air. Its territory includes three smaller islands, Mona to the west and Culebra and Vieques (VYAY-kess) to the east. With close to three million people in an area of 3,435 square miles (not much bigger than Delaware, and a good bit of it too mountainous to live on), it is crowded and growing more so.

Puerto Rico is unique politically. In 1952, after half a century as an American possession (acquired from Spain in the war over Cuba), it became a commonwealth.* Puerto Ricans are American citizens but pay no federal income tax and cannot vote in national elections. They choose their own governor and legislature and have a supreme court appointed by the governor, which may be overruled by the Supreme Court in Washington. Puerto Rico uses American money and postal service. Its youths are subject to the draft. It celebrates ten American holidays—and nine of its own.

Puerto Rico wrote the economic success story called Operation Bootstrap. This is the continuing program, begun in 1948, to attract industry to an island of poor farmers. It has worked so well that today Puerto Rico almost bristles with factories and the things

* The Puerto Rican name for it may be better: *Estado Libre Asociado* (Es-TA-doe LEE-bray A-so-SYA-doe), meaning Associated Free State.

114 HELLO, WEST INDIES

they make possible: housing, schools, highways, autos, supermarkets, bank accounts, and much more. Income per person is the highest in Latin America, though lower than in any American state.

Puerto Rico is where one of the great migrations of recent years began. Though Operation Bootstrap created many jobs, hundreds of thousands of Puerto Ricans still left to seek work on the mainland. Settling at first mainly in New York, they created a huge minority group whose presence now is felt all across the country.

Puerto Rico is the most popular single tourist island in the Antilles. Its appeal has been heavily publicized as part of Operation Bootstrap, and helped by Fidel Castro's closing off of Cuba. Most visitors stay close to San Juan, where luxury hotels line nearly two miles of the Atlantic shore. They miss many other attractions, including the central mountains that rise to 4,350 feet and are laced by good roads affording superb views; the island's second and third cities, Ponce (POAN-say) on the south coast and Mayagüez (Maya-GWESS) on the west; the rain forest of El Yunque (YOONkay), with roadside waterfalls used by young men for washing their cars on Sundays; the arid southwestern "cactus belt"; the area of limestone sinks, one cupping the world's largest radio-radar telescope (1,000 feet in diameter); hundreds of miles of beaches, open by law to everyone; and above all, the chance to meet people who are among the friendliest anywhere.

Even Puerto Rico's background is distinctive: it was the only Spanish colony in the hemisphere that never rebelled against Spain. Relations with the mother country stayed tolerable from the appearance of Juan Ponce de León in 1508 to the landing of American troops in 1898. The Americanization of the island began at once, but has yet to erase traditional ways of thinking and behaving. As just one example, the Spaniards rarely discriminated by skin color. There were Negro slaves (today one islander in ten is black, and about half the rest are mulatto) but, once freed, they received the same political and social rights as everyone else. Most Puerto Ricans are outraged by discrimination as practiced on the mainland.

Conflicts and contrasts between old and new are routine in

PUERTO RICO 115

Puerto Rico. Take language. Everyone speaks Spanish,* but English is a required subject all through school. Laws are printed in both. The island has three daily newspapers in Spanish, one in English; radio and TV stations follow a similar pattern. Many people use an idiomatic Spanish containing so many English words that some call it Spanglish. An example is the invitation often posted in stores: "*Use nuestro* easy lay-away plan." The first two words are Spanish and mean "Use our." The rest are English because "easy lay-away plan" is almost untranslatable.

Or take El Morro, the great fort at the entrance to San Juan· Harbor. The Spaniards built it as a defense against pirates, and it proved its worth in 1595 when Sir Francis Drake swept in. El Morro's gunners repelled him with cannon fire so accurate that one shot hit Drake's cabin, killed two men, and barely missed Drake himself. El Morro served Spain well on other occasions. But today it is run by the National Park Service for visiting *turistas*.

When San Juan was founded in 1521, it was called Puerto Rico or Rich Port. The island as a whole had been named for San Juan Bautista, St. John the Baptist, by Columbus. Later the names got switched around, no one seems sure why. As a colonial capital, San Juan was only some seven blocks square, on a small island dominated by El Morro and other forts. Much of the city eventually fell into decay. Today, thanks to a major restoration program, Old San Juan looks much as it once did. The streets are straight and narrow, some paved with *adoquines* (a-doe-KE-nace), shiny blue-gray bricks brought from Spain as ships' ballast. Buildings feature long balconies, wide entrance halls, inside patios. Many of them now house shops or art galleries. Restaurants offer American food or such Puerto Rican standbys as *asopao* (a thick, spiced soup of rice with chicken or seafood), *lechón asado* (roast suckling pig), *tostones* (fried plantain slices), and guava paste with white cheese for dessert.

As San Juan spread beyond its original island, the time came when a trolley line was needed. Its stops were numbered in sequence, and people would use a stop number to mean the area

* Many Latin Americans call average Puerto Rican Spanish the worst spoken in the hemisphere. It is rapid, slangy, and marked by such mispronunciations as changing the letter *r* to *l* (as in Puelto Lico).

around it. "I'm going to visit my cousin Graciela," they might say, "at Stop Eleven." Some *sanjuaneros* still do this although the trolleys are long gone.

Some residents today may have trouble recognizing their city at all. Operation Bootstrap brought people from all over the island to look for work and material comforts. In a few years the capital unrolled for miles south, east, and west. Former suburbs were engulfed. Former open land sprouted low- and middle-income housing. Except for the tropical planting, most of the newer San Juan could be a mainland city. Boulevards and expressways face flooding traffic. (The number of cars in Puerto Rico tripled from 1960 to 1970.) Air-conditioned buses glide past air-conditioned office

Old San Juan: El Morro Fort still guards the headland that creates the capital's harbor (right). The old city lies in the background. At far left, facing the ocean, is La Perla, a small but noted slum.

New San Juan: Gleaming modern buildings form the nucleus of a new financial and commercial center in Hato Rey, southeast of the old city. This view is northward toward high-rise buildings on the coast.

buildings and factories. Students demonstrate on the tree-shaded campus of the University of Puerto Rico (total enrollment about 35,000). But outside the gates is an island tradition: street venders selling *piraguas,* shaved ice sweetened with syrup.

New housing is eliminating San Juan's slums, once among the worst in the hemisphere. Filthy, overcrowded, disease ridden, they were created largely by thousands of rural families that streamed into the capital in the 1920's and 1930's. The *jíbaro* (HE-ba-ro) or small farmer often could not compete with the big sugar, coffee, and tobacco plantations. There simply was too little land to go around, even too little for the *jíbaro* to feed his family. Things might be bad in the capital, but a skilled needlewoman, as many Puerto Rican wives were then, might find temporary work hemming handkerchiefs, say, at 15 cents a dozen.

Looking back, it is hard to understand America's indifference to all this. But we had paid scant attention to the island after annexing it in 1898. Puerto Ricans received American citizenship in 1917. They elected their own legislature, but it could be overruled

118   HELLO, WEST INDIES

by governors sent from Washington. Not until the depression of
the 1930's did our government start serious study of Puerto Rican
problems. A long-range development program began only in the
1940's. The idea for it came not from Washington but from a
remarkable Puerto Rican, Luis Muñoz Marín (Lu-EECE Mu-
NYOCE Ma-REEN), son of another remarkable man, poet-poli-
tician Luis Muñoz Rivera.

The elder Muñoz * was the Puerto Rican version of a revolutionary patriot—that is, he championed autonomy for the island
under Spanish rule. After ten years of effort, he won from Spain
an enlightened charter that granted Puerto Rico a large measure
of self-government. Ironically, it went into effect in 1897. The
next year, American troops came ashore at dusty Guanica (WA-
ne-ca) on the south coast and changed the course of island history.

Most Puerto Ricans welcomed the change. They admired the
American system of government and expected good things from
it. Many assumed that Puerto Rico, like Wyoming or Utah, would
become an incorporated territory, then a state. It became neither.
Indeed, it fell into the fuzzy category of "possession."

Then along came Luis Muñoz Marín, a heavy-set man with a
mustache—and an idea. Like his father, he was both a poet and a
politician. Born in San Juan, he grew up in Washington, D.C.,
when his father was representing Puerto Rico there, and later lived
in New York City. After returning to the island, he publicly supported Puerto Rican independence. Then he got his idea. Briefly, it
was that the island's political status could wait until more pressing
human needs—land, schooling, jobs—were met. In 1938 he
formed the Popular Democratic Party to push for that. In the 1940
election it won control of the island legislature.

Muñoz's idea largely marked time during World War II, but
with peace he swung into high gear. Originally most anxious about
the *jíbaros,* he now felt the whole island must move ahead together,
and industry was the key. After experiments with government-
owned factories that lost money, he set in motion a program to
attract mainland investors.

* In Spanish-speaking lands, a child generally uses both his father's and his mother's
family names, the father's first. The mother of Luis Muñoz Rivera was a Rivera.
The mother of Luis Muñoz Marín was a Marín. Both men may be called Muñoz.

PUERTO RICO 119

This was Operation Bootstrap, so named because it began with very little and aimed for nothing less than the transformation of Puerto Rico. It was an island effort, though Washington at last was giving support.

In 1948 the islanders were allowed to elect their own governor. They chose Muñoz Marín. He pushed hard at the idea of making Puerto Rico a commonwealth, and in 1952 the islanders so voted. However, a minority favored statehood, and a few wanted independence. (The cause of the *independentistas* had not been helped in 1950 when some of them tried to assassinate President Harry Truman.)

Puerto Rico now moved ahead under the PDP, with Muñoz re-elected governor three times. In 1964 he retired, leaving a big gap in island life. His successor was another PDP choice, Roberto Sánchez, but in 1968 a strong supporter of statehood, industrialist Luis Ferré (Fair-RAY), was elected.

None of this affected Operation Bootstrap, which has achieved more than perhaps even Muñoz expected. Most of its thrust came through the Economic Development Administration, generally called *Fomento* (Development, in Spanish). *Fomento* promoted Puerto Rico as a great place to build factories. It stressed that plenty of labor was available, at pay scales much lower than on the mainland, and that Puerto Ricans were hard, able workers. Further, manufacturers were guaranteed freedom from income or property taxes for ten years (later extended to as long as 17 years).

It added up to a convincing argument. American firms responded favorably. Within a few years they were building an average of six new plants a month in Puerto Rico. A recent survey showed that *Fomento* had helped bring in more than 1,500 factories (including expansion of existing ones) that employ more than 100,000 Puerto Ricans.

Operation Bootstrap telescoped decades of industrial progress into a few years. In the late 1940's, local industry still was mostly processing agricultural products, such as cane into sugar. In the 1950's came light industry, with materials and components sent from the mainland to be worked into clothing, shoes, textiles, electrical and electronic items.

The 1960's and 1970's brought heavy industry. Factories, mills,

120   HELLO, WEST INDIES

and refineries began turning out such things as metal products, machinery, and chemicals. Particularly impressive is a petrochemical complex on the south coast near Ponce, where several oil companies have invested hundreds of millions of dollars. Essentially, their plants break down crude oil (largely from Venezuela) into its basic components and reassemble them into chemical "building blocks"—benzene for detergents, insecticides, and cosmetics; toluene for paints and lacquers; cyclohexane for nylon; and many more. The petrochemical plants give Puerto Rico something it never had before, a major source of raw materials, the kind today's technology needs.

If Operation Bootstrap thus is changing the face of Puerto Rico, many old customs remain. As elsewhere in Latin America, the family is the heart of Puerto Rican life. "Family" normally takes in not just parents and children but grandparents, uncles, aunts, and cousins as well—sometimes dozens of them. They consult one another on everyday decisions, visit one another incessantly, turn out in numbers when one takes a plane to the mainland or comes back.

Another big influence from Spanish days is the Catholic Church. Every community has a patron saint and celebrates his (or her) day with religious observances and, usually, an open-air fair. On Christmas Eve many people attend midnight mass, then go home for a big family supper. Parties mark the holiday season through January 6, Three Kings Day. That traditionally is the day when children receive presents, but islanders now tend to follow the mainland pattern of gifts (plus trees, ornaments, and so on) on December 25.

Catholic teaching must compete with folk beliefs and superstitions. Many people believe in witchcraft. Small stores called *botánicas* sell herbs, candles, amulets, and other items that supposedly can bring the buyer luck or help him with a problem. A very popular good-luck charm is the *azabache* (a-sa-BA-chay), a round, polished black stone or a tiny black plastic hand. It can be attached to a child's clothing to ward off the "evil eye" by intercepting the harmful look and breaking, thus protecting its wearer. Persons with larger needs may call on a spiritist to enlist the help of spirits (good or bad). The spiritist may cast a spell using oil, powder, or other items from a *botánica*. Or he may invoke the aid

PUERTO RICO 121

of Christian saints, angels, or devils to work in his behalf.

Religious feelings produced Puerto Rico's only folk art, the carving of small wooden images called *santos* or saints. There used to be hundreds of *santeros,* some of whom evolved individual styles and passed their skill down to sons and grandsons. Today there are almost none, but some *santos* survive in museums.

Artistically, Puerto Rico's biggest name is that of Francisco Oller (O-YAIR), who died in 1917. Oller studied in Paris, became a friend of many French Impressionists, painted a portrait of novelist Emile Zola that hangs in the Louvre, and came home to do his most famous work, a huge canvas of rural life called *The Wake*.

Some of the island's musical and theatrical figures are world famous; pianist Jesús María Sanromá, for example, or actor José Ferrer. Puerto Rico also can claim the remarkable cellist-conductor Pablo Casals, who was born in Spain but made the island (his mother's birthplace) his home.

Creative activities in every line are encouraged by the Institute of Puerto Rican Culture. This unusual government agency carries on dozens of programs to conserve and develop island music, dance, theater, and the like. It has charge of the restoration of Old San Juan, and itself has restored such landmarks as the foundation of Governor Ponce de León's first house, a seventeenth-century church in the southwestern town of San Germán, and an Arawak ball ground in the central mountains.

Prehistoric ball players were the spiritual ancestors of the thousands who today make Puerto Rico one of the most baseball-minded areas on earth. Boys can start as sandlotters and Little Leaguers, play all through school, and graduate to amateur leagues that blanket the island. Many men continue to play into their forties and fifties. As for the professionals, the island's six-team league plays a full winter season, after which quite a few players fly north to join major-league teams. Among them recently have been Orlando Cepeda, Roberto Clemente, Felix Millán, and others of marked ability.

Puerto Rico has other sports stars, from golf (Chi Chi Rodríguez) and tennis (Charles Pasarell) to racing (Eddie Belmonte) and boxing (bantamweight Sixto Escobar and lightweight Carlos

122 HELLO, WEST INDIES

Ortiz). But sports basically are a family affair. So, too, is education.

As recently as 1940, a third of all Puerto Ricans were illiterate. Then came Operation Bootstrap, and a sudden need for skilled workers. The government stepped up its budget to provide more schools, teachers, and classes for dropouts and adults. The first wave of light industries brought a heavy emphasis on manual training. As more complicated factories were built, the schools added a growing variety of vocational and technical courses.

Today the Puerto Rican school system is a good deal like those on the mainland. There *are* differences. Classes are conducted in Spanish; cafeteria lunches are heavy on rice, beans, and sausages; students generally wear uniforms (such as gray slacks and white shirts for boys, gray jumpers and white blouses for girls); American football is almost unknown; gifted students may receive scholarships even in grade school. The school building also may look different. Typically, it has long windows with horizontal louvers—but no glass.

Currently one Puerto Rican in three is attending some kind of school. Nearly one-third of the government's annual expenditure is on education. With Operation Bootstrap, it is the base of the island's astonishing progress.

Many problems remain, however. Prosperity has not reached all rural Puerto Ricans, nor indeed all urban dwellers. Overpopulation, despite government-approved family planning, threatens ever greater traffic jams, housing shortages, air pollution—all the things we might think a tropical island might avoid.

And the island itself keeps asking the question: What is Puerto Rico? Some feel it must become a state and merge into the American mainstream. A growing number want independence, a completely Puerto Rican identity. A big middle group so far prefers the commonwealth arrangement. Almost anything seems possible.

What is Puerto Rico? Time will tell.

13

THE VIRGIN ISLANDS

On his second voyage, in 1493, Christopher Columbus put in at an island a bit southeast of Puerto Rico. It was small—about 28 miles long—and he named it Santa Cruz or Holy Cross. After killing a few Caribs, he set sail northward toward other, even smaller islands.

These were dry and hilly, with many bays and beaches, and so numerous that they reminded Columbus of the legend of St. Ursula. One version of the legend says that Ursula, daughter of a king of Brittany, fled to sea rather than marry a pagan king, and was accompanied by no less than 11,000 other maidens. In honor of her goodly group, Columbus named his discovery the Virgin Islands.

Today the Virgins are counted as about 100 islands, cays, and named rocks. With one exception, Columbus's Santa Cruz, off to the south, they lie in a close-packed arc starting about 35 miles east of Puerto Rico and curving about 55 miles northeast. The main islands, west to east, are St. Thomas, St. John, Tortola (Tor-TO-la), Virgin Gorda, and Anegada (A-ne-GA-da). They are handsome but only sometimes green: rainfall is spotty and unreliable. Most of the other islands are too small and dry to be inhabitable. Altogether, the Virgin Islands contain only 192 square miles and about 75,000 predominantly black people. They mark the start of the Lesser Antilles, which stretch east and south to Trinidad.

Despite Columbus, the islands received scant attention from the Spaniards. The Caribs had mined a little copper on Virgin Gorda, and the conquistadors soon finished that. Then they moved on. Before long, pirates began using the Virgins' many sheltered coves

124 HELLO, WEST INDIES

and channels. English-speaking ones bestowed the salty names many islands still bear: Rum, Dead Chest, Fallen Jerusalem, Cockroach. The main stretch of water between St. John, Tortola, and Virgin Gorda is called Sir Francis Drake Channel. (He sailed through in 1585.) In it are three islets known companionably as Great Dog, West Dog, and George Dog.

Later came European settlers, including Frenchmen who translated Santa Cruz to St. Croix (now pronounced Croy). They planted sugarcane and thrived until the end of slavery. The ensuing economic collapse is only now being erased with the help of tourist dollars.

Along the way, the Virgin Islands were divided. One part became British; the other, Danish. The separation still exists, but the Danish part now is American.

The United States Virgin Islands

Westernmost in the group, closest to Puerto Rico, the American Virgins have two-thirds of the total area and five-sixths of the population. They include about 50 islands, but only three are important: St. Thomas, St. John, and St. Croix.

They are special on several counts. They have been under seven flags—one more than Texas. One of the flags belonged to the Knights of Malta, a religious-military order that bought St. Croix in 1651 from the French and sold it back 14 years later. In 1733 the King of France, needing money, sold St. Croix to the Danish West India Company, which already had colonies on St. Thomas and St. John.

The Danes turned St. Croix into a major sugar producer. With slaves brought in by the thousand, many planters became wealthy. Two towns grew up, Christiansted and Frederiksted. In Christiansted, a teenager named Alexander Hamilton clerked six years in a store before moving on to the American colonies and the spotlight of history.

Except for brief English occupations during the Napoleonic wars, the Virgins stayed Danish for two and a half centuries. After about 1820 the sugar market declined, production fell, planters

The harbor of Charlotte Amalie, capital of the United States Virgin Islands, reveals the charm the island of St. Thomas has for both cruise-ship passengers and yachtsmen. The city itself is at right.

went deeply into debt or simply quit, and the islands entered on hard times. After emancipation, labor disputes developed. In 1878 the plantation workers rioted and burned most of Frederiksted.

All this time a rescuer was standing by: the United States. Attracted by the strategic harbors of St. Thomas and St. John, our government tried to buy both islands in 1867. In 1902 we offered to take St. Croix as well. Both times the Danish government refused. When World War I broke out, it seemed possible that Germany would seize the almost undefended islands as a submarine base. We therefore raised our offer and in 1916 the Danes accepted. The following year, the Virgin Islands became American at the cost of $25 million.

For quite a while they continued to look Danish, particularly in the towns. Charlotte Amalie (A-MAHL-yeh) on St. Thomas, the territorial capital, drowsed along the bases of three hills rising steeply from a fine, sheltered harbor. Three main streets paralleled

126 HELLO, WEST INDIES

the waterfront, connected by shorter ones that headed up the hills, then stopped. Houses were comfortable, large, and airy. Merchants did business in leisurely style while their wives shopped.

Bit by bit people learned American ways. They were given citizenship in 1927. They learned to speak English, though other languages still may be heard. Baseball became the favorite sport, and a few islanders made it to the major leagues. Most took kindly to hot dogs, hamburgers, and milkshakes, though they still like their own food: fish pudding, kalaloo (a thick fish-and-vegetable soup), fungi (cornmeal balls), and others.

One American custom was rejected: driving on the right. Virgin Islanders had driven on the left as far back as anyone could remember (some say the French started it), and the story goes that their horses and mules refused to switch. So the Virgins remain the one American possession where everyone, by law, keeps to the left.

The U.S. Department of the Interior is responsible for the territory, but the islanders have had an increasing say in running it. In 1970, after years with an elected legislature and governors appointed in Washington, they began electing the governor as well. Their first choice was Dr. Melvin Evans, a black physician; his lieutenant governor, David Maas, was white.

Islanders cannot vote in presidential elections and have no representative in Congress, but they are greatly favored in monetary terms. All federal taxes collected from them are turned over to the island government. Washington adds millions of dollars a year in grants and donations. As one result, local taxes are low.

Then there is the growing tourist revenue, based largely on the fact that the Virgin Islands are the only free port on American soil. Originally a Danish idea, this means that a variety of merchandise may be imported with little or no payment of duty, and resold at correspondingly low prices. Cameras, watches, chinaware, clothing, perfume, and other items are offered at a good deal less than on the mainland. Bargain-conscious tourists have responded in droves. They come by sea (more cruise ships stop at St. Thomas than anywhere else on earth) and by air (direct from the mainland or by shuttle from Puerto Rico). They have helped transform Charlotte Amalie. The downtown area now contains block after

THE VIRGIN ISLANDS   127

block of smart shops, bargain stores, good and bad restaurants, bars, night clubs, and an atmosphere not unlike New York City's Greenwich Village. The old Danish names still grace some streets —Kongens Gade, Gamle Nordsidevei—but others now are called such things as Palm Passage and International Plaza.

The rest of St. Thomas has changed in another way. It has become a magnet for retired mainlanders. Attracted by year-round sun and outdoor living, they have been snapping up available land and building houses in which to grow old. Many have bought apartments in new condominiums (buildings owned cooperatively by the tenants). Houses and condominiums dot the winding, narrow roads that lead up and around the flanks of St. Thomas.

The island peaks yield striking views. Beaches rim blue-green bays below. (Unlike Puerto Rico's, many of these bays are privately owned and charge admission.) Off to the northeast other islands rear like half-submerged camels. The waters below normally are dotted with sails, for the trade wind blows almost without pause, pushing native fishermen and delighting yachtsmen. Westward, Puerto Rico is clearly visible.

Close to the east lies St. John, smallest and quietest of the American Virgins. It once grew sugar, but that collapsed. St. John thereafter was almost deserted except for a few descendants of former slaves. Few outsiders even knew of its beaches and clear water, tropical trees and sugar-mill ruins. In 1952 it was spotted by multimillionaire Laurance Rockefeller, who decided that such unspoiled charm should be preserved. At his urging, Rockefeller family funds were used to buy up 9,485 acres, three quarters of the island. Turned over to the federal government, it became the Virgin Islands National Park. The park's camping, swimming, hiking, and other facilities have grown so popular that reservations usually must be made a year ahead.

St. John also is where American scientists in 1970 began serious studies of man's ability to live and work on the sea floor. Their base was *Tektite 2*, a steel chamber with facilities for eating, sleeping, and other daily activities. Lowered off the island coast, it permitted underwater experiments at various depths.

Southward from St. Thomas and St. John, the solitary island of St. Croix is distinct from either (and nearly twice as big as both

128   HELLO, WEST INDIES

together). Except for the hilly northwest, into which a small but genuine rain forest is tucked, St. Croix is largely flat. Marks of its sugar history are everywhere. Fields of cane stand uncut and turning wild. Deserted mills freckle the landscape. Maps still show plantation names from optimistic (Contentment, Love, Profit) to pessimistic (Jealousy, Humbug) and one that defies explanation—Slob. Much of this land has been developed into housing for island businessmen and mainland retirees.

Among St. Croix's features are well-preserved Danish buildings in Christiansted; the underwater scenery at nearby Buck Island, a national monument, where signs below the surface explain corals and fishes to snorkelers floating above; and East Point, a windswept rocky area of cactus and tough brush, which is the easternmost spot under the American flag. St. Croix also has the main results so far of the Virgin Islands' effort to attract industry. They include a refinery that processes imported oil, a plant that processes imported bauxite, and a factory where workers assemble imported parts into watches.

Actually, between tourists and tax benefits the islanders do quite well. Their income per person is the highest in the West Indies. The slum shacks so conspicuous in Jamaica or Haiti have been largely replaced by modern housing. Everyone is familiar with supermarkets, drive-in movies, air conditioning, and television. Hospitals and health care are excellent. The perennial water problem is being overcome. Where once the islanders depended on roof cisterns and big hillside catchments for rainwater, they now can call on desalting plants that make seawater drinkable.

Island education, once only fair, has improved. Buses now bring pupils from every spot on each island to centrally located schools. The College of the West Indies, established in 1965, offers four-year courses. It has campuses on St. Thomas and St. Croix.

Work is plentiful on the islands. Tourism gives jobs to many. So does the construction of hotels, homes, and housing. The island government is a big employer. (Too big, critics say.) This is almost the only place in the Antilles with more jobs than workers. Though many of the jobs are menial—dishwashers, trash collectors, and the like—aliens from other islands (chiefly former British colonies) seem eager to fill them. Lately, aliens have made up

THE VIRGIN ISLANDS 129

close to half the total work force of these tourist-flooded islands.

The other side of the picture is less pleasing. Criticism is widely heard that Virgin Islanders have things *too* easy. For example, when the College of the V.I. offered a course in hotel and restaurant management, 23 students enrolled. All but three were from outside the Virgin Islands—and none of the three finished the course, Again, some people on St. Croix refuse jobs in the oil refinery because, they say, they are afraid of fire. "Huh!" a local resident snorts. "Dey afraid of work!"

Because practically everything on the islands must be imported, including food, clothing, and other essentials, living costs are about a quarter higher than on the mainland. An islander pays $15,000 or more for a three-bedroom concrete-block house in a government development on St. Thomas. A bit farther out, mainland retirees find land costing up to $30,000 an acre, with no apparent limit on house prices. Construction materials are so expensive that one builder got the idea of prefabricating homes on the mainland and shipping them down in sections. A four-bedroom house, reassembled, still cost the buyer nearly $70,000.

High prices infuriate some black islanders because, they say, the money goes to white landlords, storekeepers, and so on. Other blacks complain of being refused service by businesses catering to white tourists. Whatever the truth in such charges, the Black Power movement has won supporters and may well win more.

The islands' future depends a good deal on what kind of government they get. Recently some officials have been criticized on grounds ranging from inefficiency and hiring unnecessary people to taking graft and mishandling public funds. In political arguments, there is a tendency for St. Thomas and St. Croix residents to take sides against each other. Politicians have to try to keep everyone happy, not an easy task. (Governor and Mrs. Evans started out right by spending part of each week on St. Thomas and the rest on St. Croix.)

Another sore spot has been the treatment of alien workers. Though essential to the island economy, they often have not shared its benefits. For lack of housing they have lived in shacks. For lack of schooling their children have gone uneducated. Such things can cause feelings that may explode into violence.

Some Virgin Islanders think their problems would be solved, or at least eased, if their small tropical domain became a state. Whether Congress ever would approve that is doubtful. Many islanders like things pretty much as they are. Hardly anyone seems to want independence. Whatever happens next door in Puerto Rico, the United States Virgins will go their own way.

The British Virgin Islands

"Next door" in the other direction, the rest of the Virgin Islands fly the Union Jack. At the closest point, their Great Thatch Island is only a few hundred yards from St. John. Anyone crossing the channel from shore to shore must follow the official procedure of clearing one country and entering another.

This artificial division strikes many people on both sides as unrealistic. The British Virgins actually are largely integrated with the American islands. They use our currency. (Their stamps are the only ones anywhere to show the British sovereign's portrait alongside a value in American cents.) Very much the same kind of

Quiet and almost empty, this street in Roadtown, capital of the British Virgin Islands, contrasts with the bustle of the American Virgins. Lately, tourist activity also has been on the rise here.

THE VIRGIN ISLANDS   131

people live on both sides, and the British Virgins supply a lot of the labor needed on the American Virgins.

The British group runs to about 50 islands, cays, and rocks, 13 of them inhabited. Their total area is 59 square miles, about the size of Salt Lake City, Utah. The biggest island, Tortola, lies directly north and northeast of St. John. On it are the islands' capital, Roadtown, and about two-thirds of their 15,000 people. Most are not only black but poor, dependent on farming or cattle raising (both in turn dependent on chancy rainfall), fishing, and money sent home from the American Virgins. Recently the tourist flood washing over the latter has lapped onto the British side as well, and several hotels have gone up on Tortola and nearby islands. With them are coming other signs of progress: airports, roads, resort homes, new businesses.

Across Drake's channel to the east is Virgin Gorda. Here the Spaniards once mined copper. Today it is the site of an elegant, isolated hotel that gets some of its water by barge from Puerto Rico.

North of Virgin Gorda is relatively remote Anegada. The channel between is tricky, much of it occupied by an extensive coral reef that rises very near the surface. Many Spanish treasure ships headed for the Atlantic ran onto this reef. Diving for doubloons is a popular pastime off Anegada.

The British Virgins were part of Columbus's tribute to St. Ursula, but the Spaniards and everyone else (except pirates) avoided them for a couple of centuries. Eventually, English settlers came and brought slaves to work sugar plantings. They were neither very numerous nor very successful. Britain made the islands a colony and administered it from London. After the slaves were freed, practically all the whites moved away. The black population hung on.

Today the islands face better prospects than ever before. Their status has been changed from colony to territory, giving the islanders more control of their own affairs. But most local couples hedge their bets on the future. If possible, they go to St. Thomas to have their babies. A child born on American soil has dual citizenship until age twenty-one. Then he can stay British or become American.

14

THE NETHERLANDS ANTILLES

The most unlikely island combination in the West Indies is the Netherlands Antilles. Dutch in government, about 90 percent black or mulatto in population, there are six of them in two groups of three each, separated by more than 500 miles of open sea. The Dutch Windwards, three volcanic dots, lie about 100 miles east of the Virgin Islands and largely surrounded by British and French possessions. The Dutch Leewards, only a little bigger, are far southwest off Venezuela, isolated from the rest of the Lesser Antilles.*

The two groups are divided by more than geography. The Windwards—Sint Maarten, Saba (SAY-ba), and Sint Eustatius, often called the Three S's—stand high and normally get ample rain. The flatter, hotter Leewards—Curaçao, Aruba, and Bonaire, often called the ABC's—are so dry that their main vegetation is cactus and scrub brush. The Windwards have no industry and only recently discovered tourism. The Leewards boast two major oil refineries and have been a prime tourist attraction for years.

On all six islands Dutch is the official tongue, but almost no one speaks it. School classes are held in Dutch, government documents are printed in it, businessmen sometimes use it. But on the Three S's people normally speak English. And on the ABC's the local

---

* A number of small islands lie eastward along the coast from the Dutch Leewards. All are part of Venezuela.

THE NETHERLANDS ANTILLES 133

language is Papyamentu (often spelled Papiamento), which has its own grammar and includes words of Portuguese, Spanish, Dutch, English, Arawak, and African origin.

This linguistic hash traces originally to the fact that the Dutch were latecomers in the West Indies. Their first formal sign of interest was formation of the Dutch West India Company in 1621. (They had moved into the East Indies 19 years before.) The Antilles already were claimed by various powers, but the Dutch got footholds on six islands and then had to fight for them. Some were captured repeatedly, usually by the English, and so acquired foreign tongues. Slaves also affected the way the whites talked. Finally, the Dutch were traders rather than empire builders, and they welcomed practically any foreigner who came in peace. So many eventually came that some 50 nationalities now are represented on Curaçao.

Most of the time they get along well together. One reason is that the islands are largely self-governing. Despite their modest area (390 square miles) and population (about 225,000) they are equal partners in the Kingdom of the Netherlands with the mother country and Surinam, the former Dutch Guiana, in South America. This was proclaimed in 1954 when the Dutch government, having lost its East Indian empire to the Indonesians, decided to give its American possessions virtual freedom. The Dutch sovereign rules all three, and the Netherlands is responsible for the defense of all. Beyond that they are largely on their own.

The capital of the Netherland Antilles is Willemstad (VIL-em-stahd) on Curaçao, the biggest island. More than half the people live on Curaçao, including the Crown-appointed governor. His position is chiefly ceremonial, but he does choose the government ministers, who in turn elect one of their number minister-president. The choices must be approved by the Staten (STAHT-en), the island's elected parliament. Its 22 members are allotted by population: 12 to Curaçao, eight to Aruba, one to Bonaire, one to the three Windwards.

To most visitors, Curaçao means Willemstad. Its main industry, a huge oil refinery, announces itself miles away by tall smokestacks and waste-gas flares. Started in 1915, the refinery gave jobs not only to local workers but also to thousands from other West Indian

134   HELLO, WEST INDIES

islands. Then automation cut back employment—so the government turned to tourism. Willemstad's first luxury hotel was built in 1957, and others have followed.

The city already was well known to cruise-ship passengers. Like many other Antillean resorts, it offered shopping bargains at free-port prices. In addition, it had something unique: what looks like a Dutch city of the early 1700's. This was when most of the original Willemstad was built, and homesickness must have played a part. Block on block was filled with the narrow three-story buildings, gabled, roofed with red tile, and painted in a rainbow of colors, that were (and are) typical of such Dutch cities as Amsterdam. As Willemstad grew, most of this waterfront area was preserved and eventually taken over by retail shops. Today, when a shipload of tourists docks, some pause to admire the buildings while the rest rush inside to scramble for enticing buys.

"Old" Willemstad is split by a deep-water channel, 500 feet wide, that leads from the sea to a sheltered inner harbor and the refinery. One side of the channel is called Punda, or Point. The other side is called Otrabanda, or Other Side. They long were connected only by a famous bridge that floated on pontoons and swung aside to let ships through. Tourists loved this. But because it happened up to 20 times a day, each time freezing land traffic for half an hour, a more efficient bridge finally was added. This carries cars 180 feet above the water and ships slide underneath.

In Punda is a side channel where boats from Venezuela (38 miles away) sell fresh fruits and vegetables at dockside. Being so close, Venezuela has had a lot to do with Curaçao. It supplies the crude oil for the refinery. Thousands of Venezuelans live or work on the island. It once gave haven to the most noted Venezuelan of all, Simón Bolívar, during his struggle to liberate his country from Spain.

From Venezuela also comes a popular menu item, the meat dumpling called a *hallaca* (a-YA-ca). But Curaçao's cuisine is global. Indonesia supplied *rijstaffel* and the less sumptuous *nasi goreng*. Another substantial dish is *keshi yena,* a whole cheese

A cruise ship steams through the main channel in Willemstad, Curaçao, where the pontoon bridge (locally called "Queen Emma") has swung back to let her pass. Old-style Dutch buildings line the opposite shore.

136   HELLO, WEST INDIES

stuffed with meat, fish, or chicken, and baked. Spiced food, unusual desserts, Chinese meals, even Dutch food—cosmopolitan Curaçao enjoys them all.

Outside Willemstad, the island is farmed after a fashion. The sparse rainfall is a constant problem, though water for domestic use now comes from one of the world's largest desalting plants. The countryside is spiky with cactus and the odd divi-divi tree. (Its bushy branches, bent by the trade wind, always point southwest.) Countrymen train one species of cactus to form living fences, useful also for hanging clothes on washday.

The Dutch took Curaçao in 1634 from the Spaniards, who had taken it in 1499 from the Arawaks, and tried to make it a plantation island. They imported slaves, built great houses, and laid out their fields. But the climate was against them. Some turned to trade, others to raising cattle and horses. Today's farmers have their own livestock: goats, which survive even on cactus.

When planting proved impractical, many colonists freed their slaves. There are fewer relics of slavery on the Dutch islands than on most others. A happy relic is a dance called the *tambú* (originally the name of a wooden drum). This brings hundreds of people together to dance, sing, and enjoy one another to the beat of the *tambú* and other rhythm makers. Much rhythm also is evident at Carnival, when costumed paraders move through the streets by thousands. With them go open trucks carrying steel bands, each in noisy competition with those ahead and behind. Curaçao celebrates many other holidays, including some of Spanish, Chinese, and Jewish origin.

Aruba, 48 miles west of Curaçao, is quiet by comparison. Closer to Venezuela, flatter, and even drier, it has little scenic appeal except for some dramatically rocky landscapes and many miles of beach. The almost constant sunshine does attract tourists. Glittering hotels have gone up, and visiting crowds (mostly American) enjoy the beaches by day and the gambling casinos by night. For tourists there isn't much else to do.

Residents might be hard pressed, too, if it were not for the refinery. About as big as Curaçao's, though run by a different company and opened later (1929), it has made work for many who otherwise might have left the island long ago.

THE NETHERLANDS ANTILLES   **137**

Aruba has one distinction: it is the only island in the Antilles where the Spaniards did not exterminate the Arawaks. The conquistadors brought along livestock, the Indians proved skillful with it, and some were put to work breeding horses and cattle. A few still were doing so when the Dutch took Aruba in 1636 and decided to let them continue. The last Arawak reportedly died in 1860, two to three centuries after his people had vanished everywhere else.

The third ABC island, Bonaire, lies 20 miles east of Curaçao. It is half again as big as Aruba, but has far fewer people and no industry. Farming and fishing are the main occupations. Local governmental needs are met in part from the national treasury. But the climate is fine, the beaches are good, the island is scenic, and tourist hotels are a-building.

The island does grow aloe, a plant whose spiked, fleshy leaves yield an extremely bitter substance with marked medicinal properties. Shortwave radio transmission also is a Bonaire business. Steel masts hundreds of feet tall send out programs from two sources, Trans World Radio (American) and Radio Netherlands (Dutch), that may be heard thousands of miles away. To nature lovers, Bonaire's prime attraction is the pink flamingos that breed by the hundreds on the muddy shores of shallow salt lagoons.

The Dutch exploited the salt "pans" at the island's flat, treeless southern end quite early. Salt then was valued particularly as a preservative for meat and fish. On Bonaire it could be had just by letting the fiery sun evaporate the seawater in the pans, then collecting the salt left behind. Slaves were brought in to do the physical labor, and a brisk trade developed. Ships came to pick up the salt at loading spots which, because Bonaire is so flat, were marked by tall obelisks along the shore. The obelisks still stand. So do some of the kennel-sized huts in which the slaves slept.

Northeast across the Caribbean, salt also led to colonization of the Dutch Windwards. That began on St. Maarten, only 37 square miles in area but with a big salt lake behind a sandspit on the south shore.

Though claimed by Spain, St. Maarten was unoccupied when the Dutch landed in 1631. Two years later a Spanish force appeared and drove them off. They next tried mountainous St. Eusta-

It looks like snow, but this wheelbarrow is filled with salt from a lake on Bonaire. Once worked by slaves, later almost abandoned, the salt pans now are producing again under American direction.

tius, now generally called Statia (STAY-sha). Statia is 32 miles south of St. Maarten, covers just 11 square miles, and has no harbor; the Dutch settled on a narrow plateau above an open roadstead. A few years later they occupied an even less promising site 17 miles west, five-square-mile Saba. Essentially an extinct volcano, Saba has sides too steep for beaches and a peak usually shrouded in clouds. Settlers had to land through the surf on the rocky shore, climb the slopes, and carry or drag their possessions with them.

In 1644 a Dutch fleet from Curaçao attacked St. Maarten again. The Spaniards not only repelled the invaders but hit their leader, Pieter Stuyvesant, with a cannon ball, costing him a leg. Then the Spaniards decided to move out of St. Maarten and the Dutch came back.

French colonists arrived about the same time, and new fighting loomed until everyone agreed on a friendlier solution: divide the island. The Dutch got 16 square miles, including the salt lake. The French got 21, including a clear view of Anguilla (An-

THE NETHERLANDS ANTILLES 139

GWIL-a) to the north, where the English were settling. The French called their side Saint Martin. The division still is in effect and still friendly.

Not all was serene in the early days, however, as national rivalries waxed and waned in Europe. St. Maarten saw only one Dutch-French fight, in 1793 (the Dutch won), but at various times it was wholly controlled by one nation or the other, and at other times by the English. Before Holland's rights finally were confirmed by an 1861 treaty, St. Maarten changed hands 16 times; Saba, 12, Statia, no less than 22—and even Curaçao, five.

All this explains the use of English in the Dutch Windwards, reinforced by British and North American settlers. A clergyman from Holland, visiting St. Maarten in 1763, complained that no one there could understand him!

Whatever their origin, the Windwards islanders established themselves as smart traders. They planted tobacco, then sugar, but concluded that they could do better carrying sugar from English and French islands in Dutch ships. Statia, made a free port in the eighteenth century, became the main clearinghouse. In 1786, for example, it grew about 300 tons of sugar but shipped some 4,500 tons. Meanwhile it transshipped many other goods from Europe to North America and vice versa. English naval blockades had little effect. Statia actually funneled British munitions to the American revolutionaries. The island grew so prosperous that it was called the Golden Rock.

In November 1776 a brigantine of the new Continental Navy, the *Andrew Doria,* visited Statia. It dipped its flag and fired a salute, which shortly was answered by one from the shore—the first ever given an American warship by a foreign power.

The English took this as an insult, but got revenge five years later. England then was at war with Holland, and Admiral Sir George Rodney seized the three Dutch Windwards. On Statia he captured some 150 ships, looted goods worth about $10,000,000, destroyed considerable property, then sailed away.

Statia survived Rodney's pillage, but it could not prop up the gradually declining sugar market. Trade fell off and people began leaving. Life became quiet, then stagnant. Today only about 1,200 persons live on Statia, amid ruins of homes, warehouses, fortifica-

140 HELLO, WEST INDIES

tions, and churches. Their main hope is for tourism, and lately there have been encouraging signs. The authorities even have ordered that the resoundingly named Franklin D. Roosevelt Airport —a grass-grown landing strip—be lengthened and paved.

Nearby Saba, rising nearly 3,000 feet out of the sea, solved its flying-field problem some years ago with a paved strip on a low spur of its steep volcanic cone. The strip is only 1,300 feet long, and cliffs drop abruptly to the sea at each end, but no other place on the island was possible. It resembles an aircraft carrier's flight deck, and by law may be used by only STOL (Short Takeoff and Landing) planes that need minimum taxiing room.

From the airport an astonishing road zigzags up the island's flank, over the ridge into the central crater, across, up, over the far side and down again—only six miles altogether, but it reaches from the Atlantic to the Caribbean and connects all of Saba's small settlements. Dutch engineers said the road could not be built, but a Saban laid it out and fellow islanders placed its stones by hand.

Sabans have shown a sturdy independence from the start. Their island has demanded it of them. On occasion they fought off invaders by rolling big stones down on them. Later the islanders carved out the rock stairways, called steproads, that were their only thoroughfares until the road was made. (The longest has 964 steps and still may be climbed.) They hauled in the materials to build neat little houses, white with green trim and red roofs, and where necessary anchored them to the ground to keep them from blowing away. The men farmed Saba's volcanic soil, or went to sea, or worked in the refineries on Curaçao and Aruba. The women stayed home, and some of them became expert at a rare type of embroidery called drawn work.

Saba's villages have colorful names: Hell's Gate, Windwardside, The Bottom. The island is a few minutes by air from St. Maarten and Statia. It needs tourists to produce revenue, and is beginning to get some. For those who want the unusual, Saba is a find.

And for others there is St. Maarten. Still divided as in 1648, it was discovered by American vacationers only within the last few years and is racing to make up for lost time. With luxury hotels, free-port shopping, gambling, and so on, it fast is becoming a resort island on the order of St. Thomas. Most of the activity centers on Philipsburg, capital of the Dutch side. It lies along the sandspit between the salt lake and the harbor, and traffic crawls through on two long one-way arteries called Frontstreet and Backstreet. St. Maarten license plates say in English "The Beach Island."

Roads lead around the island to Marigot (Ma-re-GO), capital of the French side. The only way anyone knows he is crossing the border is by a simple marker and a sign welcoming him to Saint Martin or Sint Maarten, depending on his direction. Most people on both sides are black and speak English.

St. Maarten has one enterprise all its own. This is a Japanese fishing fleet that sends powerful trawlers thousands of miles out

Three centuries of peace are commemorated by this marker on the boundary between French Saint Martin (left) and Dutch Sint Maarten. Everyone crosses unimpeded by border guards or customs inspections.

142 HELLO, WEST INDIES

into the Atlantic for tuna, marlin, and other big food fish. Each trawler puts over a heavy nylon cable several miles long, with thousands of baited hooks on short side lines; it takes a day to unreel, and longer to haul in. The ships follow known fish-migration routes, spot large schools with depth sounders, and exchange information by radio. In a year, millions of pounds of fish are brought to St. Maarten to be frozen and shipped out, mostly to Puerto Rico for canning. The Oriental trawler crews relax between trips at their club near Philipsburg. There they can enjoy their favorite food: fish.

St. Maarten benefits modestly on all this by taxing fish brought in and shipped out. But the Japanese have created few jobs for local residents and spend little money ashore. Meanwhile, they are slowly but steadily fishing out the Atlantic Ocean.

Industry in the Netherlands Antilles remains concentrated in Curaçao and Aruba. Even there it has not all gone smoothly. In 1969 violence hit downtown Willemstad, particularly Otrabanda. It began as a wage strike against a contracting firm working for the refinery. Strikers and their supporters marched on government buildings, and a riot developed. Some persons were killed and more hurt, 30-odd buildings were burned, and there was looting.

Most islanders seemed to feel that this outbreak was the exception, not the rule. It had few racial overtones. Like most labor strikes, it was based on money. Later in the year there were other strikes, without rioting. And in an election for the Staten, three of Curaçao's 12 seats were taken by a leftist party called *Frente Obrero,* or Worker Front. Some of its members dressed in the style of Fidel Castro, with berets and beards. But one of their announced goals was a very un-Castrolike increase in tourism.

Behind the labor agitation is the fact that unemployment runs close to 25 percent on Curaçao and even higher on some of the other islands. It may take all the good qualities the Dutch possess to keep the Netherlands Antilles moving ahead.

15

THE ENGLISH-SPEAKING LEEWARDS

A bit southeast of the Dutch Windwards, at the northeast corner of the Lesser Antilles, lie the English-speaking Leeward Islands. Small and largely dry, with no mineral resources, they held little for their Spanish discoverers—but their location invited the English and French to move in later. Both made their first Antillean settlements here, on St. Christopher (St. Kitts). The English eventually anchored their Caribbean power on St. Kitts and nearby Antigua while the French occupied other islands to the north and south.

The three main Leewards form a rough triangle. St. Kitts and Nevis (two miles apart) are in the northwest angle, in full view of Dutch Statia; with them, for administrative purposes, the British lumped Anguilla, around to the north of St. Maarten. East of Nevis lies Antigua, with bare little Barbuda as a dependency. The south point of the triangle is Montserrat, with French Guadeloupe beyond.

St. Kitts-Nevis and Antigua are British Associated States, self-governing except for defense and foreign affairs. Montserrat is a Crown Colony with a London-appointed administrator and a local legislature. Anguilla, assigned to St. Kitts-Nevis when the Associated States were formed in 1967, promptly broke away; its status is in doubt.

The English-speaking Leewards total only 363 square miles. Their population is about 165,000, largely descended from slaves and largely dependent on tourism and agriculture.

Surrounded by palms, this Victorian clock tower is the center of Basseterre, capital of St. Kitts. Things normally are quiet here, but somewhat busier on the waterfront—which is two blocks away.

THE ENGLISH-SPEAKING LEEWARDS   145

St. Kitts-Nevis

This two-island country began with three, and its flag still bears the words "Unity from Trinity." Even the remaining two, however, are none too united.

On the map St. Kitts looks a lot like a bowling pin, its base rather chunky, its neck pointing southeast at Nevis, which, suitably, is almost as round as a bowling ball. Both islands are volcanic, rising to symmetrical central cones (long dormant) with good soil on their lower slopes. They get enough rain, and might produce varied crops. They have good beaches, and might attract tourists. But as this is written they grow almost nothing but sugarcane, and visitors are less eagerly sought than anywhere in the Antilles except Cuba.

The concentration on sugar is a legacy from colonial days, but the attitude toward tourists dates largely from 1967, when the first black government took power. Labor leader Robert Bradshaw, elected premier by the sugar workers he himself had organized, proved markedly antiwhite. White businessmen were encouraged to leave the country and new ones were not welcomed. Opponents of this policy might wind up in jail.

Bradshaw nonetheless faced opposition. Foreign whites owned most of the good sugar land, and buying it up would put the government deep in the chancy sugar business. There was little other source of employment, so the refusal to encourage tourism meant the loss of job opportunities. Bradshaw did approve one big hotel-and-housing development on St. Kitts, but the foreign investors were wary of going ahead until the political climate improved. Across the water in Nevis there was clear dissatisfaction with the way things were going.

Meanwhile both islands retained their individual flavor, which is more colonial than in most of the Antilles.

St. Kitts has a tidy British air, with French touches. French settlers named its capital and only port Basseterre (Bahss-TAIR), or Low Land. It still is small and quiet, laid out in neat rectangles, with white houses amid palm trees and scarlet poinciana (named for the first French governor, Philippe de Poincy). A red, four-sided Victorian clock tower (with a clock face on each

146   HELLO, WEST INDIES

side) graces the round central "square." Streets stop abruptly at the edge of town and canefields begin. Interisland steamers and native fishing craft are the main users of the Basseterre pier, and along the shore an open-air market functions on weekdays. Sundays, everything but churches is closed on St. Kitts. A typical sign reads, "As for my house and myself, we will serve the Lord." It is displayed on the mirror behind one of Basseterre's few bars.

English and French originally settled St. Kitts by joining to massacre the local Caribs, then outwaiting a temporary Spanish occupation. The island thereafter was divided for nearly a century. The French had both ends and the English had the center. Then the English took over and, as an expression of London's colonial ambitions, began building fortifications on Brimstone Hill, a rocky outcrop 750 feet high on the coast west of Basseterre.

Thick walled and bristling with cannon, Brimstone Hill became known as the "Gibraltar of the West Indies." Ironically, it was attacked just once—and that time it fell. It happened in 1782, when the unfinished fort was garrisoned by 1,200 men and a French force of 6,000 besieged it. The defenders held out nearly a month, so bravely that the French let them march out with flying colors and carrying their arms.

The siege was supported by a fleet under Admiral Comte de Grasse. At one point a smaller English fleet appeared to help the defenders, and the French moved out to do battle. Then the English commander, Sir Samuel Hood, pulled a sly trick. Turning southward as though fleeing, he led the French away from the shore—only to swing back and occupy the position they had vacated. De Grasse, unable to break through the English line, blockaded St. Kitts for weeks before giving up in disgust. Hood's maneuver paved the way for later English recapture of Brimstone Hill.

The fort was manned until 1854. Today, partially restored, it is a mammoth monument to Britain's vanished power and a favorite spot with visitors. The summit gives a superb view of Statia and Saba, and St. Kitts' own 3,800-foot Mt. Misery close by. There are African monkeys, descended from pets brought by slaves, on Misery's higher slopes. They come down the *ghauts* * or ravines

* Pronounced gawt (properly) or gut (by most islanders), this is a Hindu word that has spread through the English-speaking Antilles, probably from Trinidad.

THE ENGLISH-SPEAKING LEEWARDS 147

to steal sugarcane and, if caught, to grace the tables of Kittitians who like roast monkey.

The view from Brimstone Hill also includes Nevis, whose village-sized capital, Charlestown, is less than an hour from Basseterre by water and about ten minutes by air. Nevis covers only 36 square miles, but its central peak rises to 3,200 feet and almost always wears a white cloud cap. Back when Brimstone Hill was important, Nevis's sugar won it the name "Queen of the Caribbees." Today what little sugar is produced goes to St. Kitts for processing. Nevis has a shaggy, unkempt air, and the road that circles it is one of the worst main roads in the West Indies.

Nevis's glory is its history. First spotted by Columbus in 1493, it was settled in 1628 by Englishmen from St. Kitts. (The Caribs on Nevis fled southward after the St. Kitts massacre.) Despite intermittent French attacks, the colonists were able to bring in slaves and build a plantocracy. By the mid-1700's Nevis was a social center of repute, though the birth of Alexander Hamilton in 1757—and his departure for St. Croix at the age of five—attracted little attention.

Nevis was famed in those days for its hot springs. Captain John Smith and crew, bound for Virginia, enjoyed them as early as 1607. Later travelers found the waters healthful, and eventually the Bath House Hotel was built. A handsome stone structure on a hillside, it became internationally known and drew visitors from as far away as England. Today it is largely in ruins.

The airs and graces of Nevis must have appealed to a young naval captain stationed at Antigua, 40 miles east. He was Horatio Nelson, later to become the hero of Trafalgar. On Nevis he wooed a widow, Mrs. Frances Nesbit, and married her in 1787 at a great house now vanished.

Nelson previously had enraged the merchants of Nevis by seizing four American ships trading there in defiance of official regulations. Local authorities long had winked at the law and Nelson's proper action was considered almost piratical. It took a while for the matter to blow over.

Today the main memento of Nelson on Nevis is a faded entry in a church registry, recording his marriage. The church itself is small, rundown, and in need of funds. Much the same may be said of Nevis.

148　HELLO, WEST INDIES

Anguilla

With 35 square miles and some 6,000 black inhabitants, Anguilla is not an impressive island at first glance. Thin and snakelike in outline (its name means eel in Spanish), it lies 12 miles north of St. Martin and about 55 miles north of St. Kitts. Handsome beaches are Anguilla's main asset. It has no electricity except from private generators, no telephones, and almost no roads. People get by on farming, fishing, and money sent home by Anguillans working elsewhere. It is an island badly in need of outside assistance.

Yet the Anguillans are among the most vigorously independent people anywhere. When Britain created the state of St. Kitts-Nevis-Anguilla in 1967, Anguilla took an immediate dislike to the Bradshaw government on St. Kitts. Soon it voted overwhelmingly (1,813 to 5) to secede. It then asked for direct ties with Great Britain; while London hesitated, Anguilla turned to Washington and asked to become American; when our government passed the request back to Britain, the Anguillans voted again, this time for full independence. Britain belatedly sent an official to offer the direct ties originally sought. The Anguillans told him firmly to get off their island.

That was too much for Her Majesty's Government. A 300-man force was flown from London to pacify the rebels. The islanders reacted calmly. When the troops came ashore, only a few children were on hand to greet them. Anguilla's President Ronald Webster learned of the invasion from reporters sent to cover it. Webster urged his people to keep cool, and they did. The British searched everyone's house for weapons (they found none), rounded up a dozen Americans for questioning (then released them), and after a few days flew home again. The whole episode caused laughter on both sides of the Atlantic.

All of Anguilla's problems remained, but the people had made their point. *They* thought they were independent. In 1971, London promised to make it official.

THE ENGLISH-SPEAKING LEEWARDS 149

Antigua

As eager for tourists as St. Kitts is reluctant, Antigua woos them with outstanding beaches and nearly three dozen resort hotels. The island is largely flat and nearly round, but has some fine harbors. Its big lack is rainfall. Long planted to sugarcane, it now is dotted with abandoned mills.

Columbus named Antigua after a church in Seville, Spain. Englishmen from St. Kitts arrived in 1632, drove out the local Caribs, and settled in. Because of its strategic location, French and other attackers tried for Antigua until England won permanent possession by treaty. London then sent out engineers to start fortifying a sheltered body of water called English Harbour.

Building went on for more than a century, making this a naval base to match the land fortress on St. Kitts' Brimstone Hill. It provided a snug haven where fighting ships could be repaired and refitted, and their crews rested. Men-of-war from all points of the compass came and went. Hood, Rodney, and other English seadogs used the fully equipped dockyard. Horatio Nelson, captain of H.M.S. *Boreas,* spent three years at English Harbour.

Like Brimstone Hill, English Harbour was attacked only once —by French schooners from Guadeloupe in 1803. An English frigate met them outside the harbor and drove them off.

The dockyard finally was abandoned in 1889. The buildings soon decayed in the tropical climate, and by 1947 their condition was officially termed "deplorable." Then the governor formed a restoration group and raised funds in Britain and from visitors (chiefly American). Today the big dockyard looks much as it used to, with storehouses, officers' quarters, a forge, a blacksmith shop, and so on, including capstans once used to reel in lines attached to ships for careening (turning on their sides for hull cleaning or repair). Though Horatio Nelson called the place "an infernal hole," the restorers have named it Nelson's Dockyard and made it a tourist magnet.

From English Harbour it is only eight miles across Antigua to St. John's, the capital. This is a small town, neatly laid out, and usually hot. Balconies over sidewalks shade pedestrians. The lovely old Anglican cathedral stands on a rise beside a graveyard where earthquakes have made headstones lean crazily and forced coffins out of the ground. The government helps maintain the cathedral because its roof is used as a public cistern for rainwater.

When Antigua became independent in 1967, its first elected government also assumed responsibility for smaller Barbuda, 30 miles north (along with uninhabited Redonda, about the same distance west). Flat, dry, and scrub covered, Barbuda in 1691 was given outright to Christopher Codrington, governor of the Leeward Islands. Descendants of Codrington slaves are noted today as fishermen and boatmen. Barbuda's dusty capital is named Codrington. Barbuda has good hunting and fishing, and one small, very expensive hotel.

The Catholic church in St. John's, capital of Antigua, looks seaward over somewhat hilly streets and modest homes. Catholic and Anglican faiths count the highest membership on the formerly British islands.

THE ENGLISH-SPEAKING LEEWARDS 151

Back on Antigua, hotels may yet balance the budget. Lately the sugar market has been poor. The government bought up about 40 percent of the island sugar industry, but has been unable to do better with it than private owners did. Antiguans necessarily look to tourism, but they take life as it comes. One of their pastimes is racing goats, often dressing the animals in costume and even lipstick. They hold Carnival in midsummer, culminating on the first Monday in August (the day slavery was abolished in 1834). They work hard if they must and relax when they can. One symptom of this attitude is the hillocks of litter along main roads, unsightly but untouched.

A recent visitor asked about the litter. His driver looked at it without interest, then flashed a smile. "Dat's all right, sah," he said. "We ain't fussy."

Montserrat

The last English-speaking Leeward is only 27 miles southwest of Antigua, but it is strikingly different. Montserrat is volcanic, steeply mountainous, well watered, mantled with vegetation. It has cool waterfalls and a sulfurous crater, the Soufrière. It never grew much sugar, but it does grow vegetables (notably tomatoes) and fruit. It has no good harbor. Its few beaches are composed mainly of black volcanic sand. It covers 39 square miles and has about 14,000 people. Nearly a quarter of the population emigrated to the British Isles in 1954–60, looking for work. In 1970, after 15 years as head of the island government, William Bramble was voted out and replaced by the opposition-party leader—his son Austin.

Montserrat shares with Antigua the 1632 Englishmen from St. Kitts. With them came Irishmen who, with later arrivals, left some typical names (Sweeney, Fagan, and others) and a touch of Irish brogue among today's black inhabitants. With this slim tie, and its prevailing greenness, Montserrat sometimes is called the Emerald Isle.

Columbus named Montserrat for a saw-toothed mountain in Spain. The French tried to wrest it from the English, and twice

152   HELLO, WEST INDIES

succeeded. From those days dates a fort—eighteenth-century cannons still in place—above Plymouth, the capital. Even older is St. Anthony's Church, just outside Plymouth. It stands beside a time-twisted tamarind tree where worshipers once hitched their horses.

Since the early 1960's Montserrat has become the site of four separate resort-and-retirement developments. Americans, Canadians, and others have bought hundreds of building lots. Roads and utilities have been brought in, and houses of various sizes have been put up by native labor using largely imported materials. It all means money in circulation. How it will affect the people of Montserrat may be another matter.

16

THE FRENCH WEST INDIES

When the European colonial powers were dismantling their empires after World War II, France let go everything in Africa and Asia but kept her West Indian possessions. Long regarded as practically part of the mother country, they officially were made so in 1946. The two largest, Guadeloupe and Martinique, became overseas departments—the equivalent of states in America. Exactly like those in France, each is run by a prefect (governor) appointed in Paris, with an elected local council (legislature). Each also sends two senators and three deputies (congressmen) to the French parliament.

Guadeloupe lies about 35 miles southeast of Montserrat (and about 3,800 miles southwest of Paris). Its 687 square miles make it the biggest island between Puerto Rico and Trinidad. It has some small island dependencies near by, and two others well to the northwest. About 85 miles south of Guadeloupe lies Martinique, smaller (431 square miles) but with slightly more people (about 350,000). British Dominica sits between Guadeloupe and Martinique, a reminder of the days when all these islands were pawns in Europe's colonial chess game.

Guadeloupe and Martinique are volcanic, with high central peaks and well-watered slopes that yield such tropical products as bananas, pineapples, coffee, and cacao. Flatter areas produce sugarcane. Sugar and bananas, with molasses and rum, make up the main exports and, for most people, the only source of employment. Martinique also grows anthurium, a waxy scarlet flower, for shipment chiefly to Europe. Both islands have some fine beaches

154 HELLO, WEST INDIES

and some good hotels. After years of catering to French Canadians, the *hoteliers* are making a strong bid for English-speaking guests.

The people of the main islands are largely descended from slaves, with a high percentage of mulattoes. The racial mixture includes two kinds of Indian blood—from the original Caribs, and from farm workers brought from India proper after slavery ended. Continuing intermarriage has made the French islands known for beautiful women, honey skinned and dark eyed.

For such women was created the *grande robe,* a costly and complicated costume now worn only on special occasions or to entertain tourists. It includes an embroidered white blouse and skirt with a tucked-up, bright-colored overskirt, a contrasting shoulder kerchief, considerable jewelry, and the famous madras headdress—a big, patterned handkerchief folded like a turban with from one to four points left sticking up. The number of points signals the wearer's interest in romance: one, she is unattached; two, she is spoken for; three, she is happily married; four, she has a man but might consider another.

Even without this outfit, French islanders dress distinctively. In the two main cities, Pointe-à-Pitre (PWANH-ta-PEETRE) on Guadeloupe and Fort de France on Martinique, young women on limited budgets are as well turned out as Parisians, while men favor shirtsleeves and sandals. Farmers work their fields in tall, conical straw hats and their wives like bright-hued bandannas.

The islands were discovered and named by Columbus, but left to the Caribs until French settlers arrived in 1635. The French fought the English for these and other islands off and on for 180 years. Guadeloupe and Martinique became noted sugar producers, and were the scene of slave uprisings during the French Revolution. One revolutionary leader, Victor Hugues, came from Paris to proclaim the end of slavery. Royalists were guillotined and confusion mounted. Napoleon temporarily restored slavery—and order.

This ornate costume is one version of the grande robe, *now worn by women of the French West Indies on special occasions. The madras headdress apparently shows that the lady is romantically unattached.*

156   HELLO, WEST INDIES

The English then occupied the islands until an 1815 treaty returned them for good.

Since then France has kept the islands dependent. They have been given good schools (by West Indian standards) where small black children begin reading lessons with such phrases as *"Je suis français"*—I am French. They have been taught the French sports of soccer and bicycle riding. (The best cyclists may cross the Atlantic for the big annual race, the 2,500-mile Tour de France.) They have learned to cook French food very well, and to frequent open-air cafés on streets named for such French notables as Victor Hugo, Ernest Renan, and Marie Curie—none of whom ever visited the West Indies.

Above all, the islanders have been encouraged to produce desirable crops—but very little else. Local factories only process farm products. Anyone needing shoes, a frying pan, or any other manufactured item must buy it with French francs from a merchant supplied, usually, from France. The islands' thousands of automobiles are almost all French. Road signs are colored and lettered exactly as in France. The single newspaper, *France-Antilles,* gets most of its contents from Paris. French magazines, paperbacks, and comic books dominate the newsstands. The single television station shows little but reruns of French programs.

All this spells profits for the merchants. Government support of prices for sugar, bananas, and so on is a boon to landowners. Government funds also have built housing for a good many families, enriching construction firms. Trade and commerce keep the two main harbors generally busy, which is good for those who own shipping, docking facilities, and the like.

Unfortunately, the people mostly benefited are members of the tiny white minority. Some money does reach the other islanders, but they still may be unemployed several months a year. Though they say *"Je suis français,"* their everyday speech is not French but Créole (as in Haiti). They may feel strongly against French landowners and France itself. When General Charles de Gaulle was premier, he spent government funds lavishly on the overseas departments, but when he visited Martinique in 1959, he was met by riots. The 1960's brought outbreaks on Guadeloupe, and French soldiers to put them down. Anyone concerned about the

THE FRENCH WEST INDIES   157

anticolonial "Third World" knows the name of Frantz Fanon, author of *The Wretched of the Earth,* who was born and reared on Martinique.

Yet the islands have many attractions even for the people who live on them. They are brilliant in sunny weather, fragrant when it rains. (Most people ignore the wet-season downpours, but many make the curious gesture of holding a newspaper, a school bag, or a bare hand protectively against their heads while their bodies are quickly soaked.) No one starves in the French West Indies, and there are many excuses for parties. Carnival, an affair of a few days on most islands, lasts six weeks on Guadeloupe and Martinique. Costumed revelers parade and party from January to Ash Wednesday, when King Carnival is buried with fitting ceremony. The Afro-French dance called the beguine is much in evidence, along with local peasant dances and rhythms from other islands.

And the average French West Indian is a warm, friendly, hospitable human being. He may not own a pair of shoes, but he likes to show off his roadside shack, his flowering trees, his family —in effect, his homeland.

Guadeloupe

Shaped in outline like a lopsided butterfly, Guadeloupe actually is two islands divided by a short saltwater channel. Illogically, the eastern island is called Grand Terre or Big Island, but is largely flat and smaller than the mountainous western island, which is called Basse Terre or Low Land.

Pointe-à-Pitre stands on Grand Terre at the southern end of the saltwater channel. It has about 60,000 residents. The older section starts immediately at the waterfront and is marked by narrow streets, colonial buildings, and crawling traffic that includes uncountable sputtering motorbikes. The block-square open-air market, colorful and odorous, is across the main street from a self-service department store. A bit farther out, older houses and slums are giving way to housing developments of striking modern design. New office buildings, schools, and medical centers help give

The open-air market in Pointe-à-Pitre, Guadeloupe, attracts shoppers who enjoy bargaining for home-grown produce arrayed on long tables. Conventional stores may be seen across the street in the background.

much of Pointe-à-Pitre an unusually up-to-the-minute look.

The countryside of Grande Terre is gently rolling, with many little hills locally called *mornes*. Sugar is the main crop. At the eastern tip of this "wing," Atlantic waves break dramatically on piled-up rocks called *chateaux* or castles. In a village along the way you might see housewives gathered for an outdoor butchering, with bloody hunks of beef or pork being wrapped in banana leaves for transport home.

A good highway leads from Grande Terre to and around Basse Terre. This "wing" is washed by the Caribbean. Its mountain spine rises to the 4,800-foot volcanic cone called, naturally, La Soufrière. Bananas and coffee are prime crops. The west coast is a

THE FRENCH WEST INDIES   159

series of cliffs broken by small beaches in a way that reminds some visitors of the French Mediterranean. Here also is the town of Basse Terre, which—rather than Pointe-à-Pitre—is Guadeloupe's capital. Though the oldest community on the island, it has only 16,000 inhabitants and is clean, quiet, and somewhat provincial. Most stores close for midday lunch and siesta. A road climbs from downtown past pleasant villas and yards full of flowers to a cooler zone of thick forest, mist, and finally the sulfur reek that says La Soufrière is alive.

Dependencies of Guadeloupe

From the southern tip of Basse Terre it is a short ride to the Îles des Saintes, eight small islands with some special features. Their people include many blond, blue-eyed whites whose ancestors were French Bretons and Normans. The men wear an odd hat—made of cloth over split bamboo, and shaped like a mushroom—that originated in Indochina. They are famous fishermen and do a good bit of smuggling. It was off the Saintes in 1782 that England's Admiral Rodney intercepted Admiral De Grasse's fleet and ended French hopes of further Caribbean conquest.

East of the Saintes is a larger island, round and flat, named Marie-Galante. It raises cotton and sugar. A bit north, off the *chateaux* of Grand Terre, is small, hilly La Désirade. It also produces cotton, and is the site of a small leper colony.

Much farther north, beyond the English-speaking Leewards, lies St. Martin, which Guadeloupe shares with the Netherlands Antilles and which we have visited briefly.

The final dependency is St. Barthélemy, commonly called St. Barts. It lies 15 miles southeast of St. Martin and 135 miles from Guadeloupe. Even smaller than St. Martin, it was settled a bit earlier and belonged briefly to the Knights of Malta. Later colonists were mainly Norman and Breton fisherfolk, as in the Saintes, and their descendants dominate among the island's 2,200 inhabitants. Older women still may wear starched white Breton-style bonnets (and go barefoot), while men may appear in long-sleeved white shirts and dark bell-bottomed trousers.

160   HELLO, WEST INDIES

For nearly a century St. Barts was Swedish. France traded it in 1784 for the right to set up a shipping base in the Swedish port of Goteborg. The Swedes named St. Barts's only town Gustavia, for their King Gustav III, and brought yellow brick to erect houses, a coaling station, and other buildings around Gustavia's small, nearly square harbor. They made it a free port, with no duties on anything. This policy was continued after the island was returned to France in 1878, and today many imported goods cost less in Gustavia than where they were made.

People trickle in from all over the Antilles to shop on St. Barts. Add sweeping beaches, fishing, and snorkeling, and the island sounds like a tourist find. But its eight square miles are windswept and bare, with water normally scarce. Jobs are so few that many islanders work elsewhere. How far St. Barts can be developed is problematical.

Martinique

Two historic events stand out on Martinique. In the late 1700's, the island sent to Paris a young lady named Marie Rose Josephine Tascher de la Pagerie, who became Napoleon's Empress Josephine and ruled over Europe's most glamorous court until the moody dictator divorced her. About a century later, Mont Pelée emitted a superheated cloud that incinerated some 30,000 persons and destroyed St. Pierre, then the island's commercial hub.

Today the center of Martinique is the capital, Fort de France, with nearly a third of the island's population. It stands on a big bay with green hills rising steeply behind. From colonial days date the remnants of a waterfront fort and a downtown area of narrow streets and close-packed buildings, many in need of repair. Along most of the sidewalks run shallow open sewers. Activities center around a four-block-square area called La Savane (Sa-VAHN), The Savanna, facing the harbor and edged with trees. Four separate soccer games often are in progress here, except when Carnival merrymakers take over. In the middle of La Savane is a statue to Josephine; on one of the bordering streets is a hotel named L'Impératrice, The Empress; in the hotel's bed-

THE FRENCH WEST INDIES 161

rooms are photos of the statue for guests who may have missed it.

Fort de France is nearly twice as big as Pointe-à-Pitre, but doesn't seem so. It is quieter, particularly after dark. There are fewer modern buildings and more signs of religious feeling— including the Church of Sacré Coeur on a hillside north of town, whose gleaming white towers copy those of the Sacré Coeur on Montmartre in Paris.

South of the capital, green *mornes* alternate with planted areas and good roads lead to a few good beaches. Off Martinique's southwest tip is Diamond Rock, England's stationary warship, looking from the shore like a misplaced haystack. Up the coast is the village of Trois Îlets (Trwah ze-LAY), site of the Pagerie plantation where Josephine spent her childhood. (She probably was born there, too, but the record is unclear.) Nothing remains from those days but a decaying sugar mill and a small museum with mementos of the onetime empress.

Relics are more numerous in St. Pierre, on the island's northwest coast. It may be approached by the shore road or by a roller-coaster inland highway over steep, rain-drenched slopes where tropical forest is broken by stands of banana and pineapple. Gradually you become aware of a looming bulk ahead: the broadshouldered, 4,583-foot Mont Pelée. At its base is what remains of St. Pierre.

Back in 1902, St. Pierre was a port city of commerce, culture, and about 35,000 inhabitants. Some had left recently, for Pelée had been rumbling and sending out lava and hot ash. But most people had stayed. The governor came up from Fort de France to assure them nothing could happen. On May 7 sympathetic tremors shook volcanic St. Vincent, 80 miles to the south, and many in St. Pierre felt that would relieve the pressure beneath Pelée. They went to bed looking forward to a street carnival, with music and dancing, the next day.

At 7:50 that morning, the side of Mont Pelée above St. Pierre blew out with a roar heard hundreds of miles away. A gigantic cloud of gas and steam hurtled down the slope and engulfed the city. Within three minutes some 30,000 persons were burned to death. One man escaped: Ludger Sylbaris, a prisoner in a thick-

162   HELLO, WEST INDIES

walled jail cell. Badly seared, he later made a living exhibiting his healed back in circus sideshows. One ship in harbor also escaped, the steamer *Roddam*. It limped to St. Lucia, next island south, with the news.

Today a little museum in the town is filled with pitiful souvenirs: melted vases, twisted spoons, stopped watches, fused metal, charred breakfast cereal. They testify to a holocaust unique in human experience. Outside the museum are bits of buildings. There is a stone entrance stairway that sweeps upward to empty space where a distinguished theater once stood.

People came back to St. Pierre. They made new homes amid the rubble and gradually the population has grown to about 4,000. Today the monster Pelée wears a placid look, almost benign. No one expects it to erupt again. But everyone knows it might.

17

THE ENGLISH-SPEAKING WINDWARDS

Four tropical islands of remarkably similar size, shape, terrain, climate, people, and history make up the English-speaking Windwards. They lie in a north-south arc, well down in the Lesser Antilles. The most northerly, Dominica, is about 25 miles north of Martinique. South from Martinique lie St. Lucia, St. Vincent, and finally Grenada, about 90 miles north of Trinidad. Between St. Vincent and Grenada (which divide their jurisdiction) is a group of very small islands called the Grenadines.

All four main islands are volcanic. Each is a rough oval, north to south, around a steep central spine with side ridges running down to the coast. Each gets abundant rainfall and is largely forested except where land has been cleared for planting. All the islands are big producers of bananas; in one recent year the four shipped out nearly two *billion* of them. Other exports include cacao, copra, spices, arrowroot, cotton, and citrus. The sugar estates of slavery days have vanished, and there is virtually no industry. But tourism is increasingly important.

The islands together cover about 820 square miles (two-thirds the size of Rhode Island) and have about 380,000 people, largely black. There is some Carib blood, and some from Indian and Portuguese laborers imported after slavery ended. Whites still own good farming land and employ many workers; others farm their own plots. All the islands are British Associated States, autonomous except for defense and foreign affairs. All have black

164   HELLO, WEST INDIES

governments. Antiwhite sentiments occasionally are heard on all.

The islands were sighted by Columbus, claimed by Spain, and colonized mainly by England and France. As the Europeans moved down the Lesser Antilles, they usually had to fight Caribs. Surviving Indians withdrew southeastward and dug in on the high, jungled Windwards, where they proved hard to dislodge. In 1797, after two years of pitched battles, some 5,000 of them surrendered to English troops on St. Vincent and were deported to small islands off the coast of Central America. (They intermarried with local Negroes, and their descendants are called Black Caribs.) Since 1903 the last few Caribs have lived in a reservation on Dominica.

Europeans in the Windwards fought each other at length. St. Lucia changed hands 14 times before British control was established. There still are forts on all the main islands, some in fair repair and armed with rusted cannon. Historic memories also linger. For one, the French Revolution inspired a black named Julien Fédon to lead a rebellion on Grenada. The lieutenant governor was captured and, with 47 others, executed. English troops crushed the outbreak, but Fédon escaped and became an Antillean folk hero.

The many changes in flag are reflected in bilingual place names, such as Fond d'Or Bay, and particularly in the *patois* spoken by almost all islanders. It is basically French, very close to the Créole of the French islands and Haiti. Many children hear English for the first time when they enter school (from which, sad to say, most still drop out before finishing sixth grade).

English influence nonetheless is strong. People drink a lot of tea, play cricket, drive on the left, run their governments on the British model. Their annual Carnival, though festive, officially lasts only two days. Visitors generally find them soft-spoken and polite, though increasingly aware of being their own bosses at last.

Dominica

Largest of the group, Dominica is the most primitive and least populated. The reason is its exceptionally rough terrain, com-

THE ENGLISH-SPEAKING WINDWARDS   165

bined with the most copious rainfall in the West Indies—from 80 inches a year at Roseau, the sea-level capital, to at least 360 inches well up the slopes of 4,747-foot Morne Diablotin. The rain packs Dominica's steep flanks and valleys with jungle trees, shrubs, hanging vines, flowers, and thick undergrowth. Hundreds of rivers and streams rush down the hillsides. In the forest live such prodigies as a six-inch cricket, a four-inch katydid, and a beetle with seven-inch wings. Much of the landscape is untouched since prehistoric times, a riot of billowing green.

Understandably, Dominica has resisted man. Land planted with bananas looks like forest. Only constant effort maintains clearings for other crops, notably limes. (The juice of Dominican limes, first used in the early 1800's on English naval vessels to prevent scurvy, gave rise to the nickname "Limey" for an Englishman.) Visitors complain at the time and expense involved in driving 35 miles across the island on the serpentine road that connects the airport and Roseau. Locals feel they should be glad there is a road there at all. Many Dominican sights—waterfalls, wildlife, sulfur pools—can be reached only by miles of soggy hiking.

Roseau is hot and sleepy, lacking both good beaches and a protected harbor. Dugout canoes and small, spritsailed fishing boats are drawn up on the waterfront. In 1908 a visitor called Roseau a "collection of shanties," and some still might. Dominicans expect better things of their other town, Portsmouth, at the far end of the island. It has beaches *and* a harbor, and was the main community until malaria drove people out. The malaria is gone now, so Portsmouth may make a comeback.

Most Dominicans live in thatched huts and eat simple food, but they have a specialty called *crapaud* (cra-PO) or "mountain chicken," actually a giant frog weighing up to two pounds. They prepare it deliciously, thanks perhaps to French instruction. A sure French legacy is the Catholic Church. Most islanders are members, though many also believe in witchcraft. Dominican men make excellent carpenters and the women are good weavers. In a Catholic convent, under the sisters' encouraging eyes, native women weave patterned grass rugs that find markets in many foreign countries.

As mentioned above, the world's last Caribs live in a Domin-

166 HELLO, WEST INDIES

ican reservation. It covers 3,700 acres on the windy Atlantic coast, a sad comedown from the 1748 treaty of Aix-la-Chapelle that awarded the Caribs the whole island. Both French and English violated the treaty, and the English finally created the reservation. It contains five scattered villages, rich but hilly farmland, and several hundred men, women, and children. The number of pure-blood Caribs is uncertain, but some of the people have strongly Indian features—almost Mongolian—that contrast sharply with those of island blacks. The reservation dwellers are poor, unlettered (though the children now go to school), and with little hope of much better—at least as Caribs. Sooner or later they seem certain to be absorbed into the Dominican mainstream.

St. Lucia

Neither so rugged nor so wet as Dominica, St. Lucia supports more people on somewhat less area. Bananas are the king crop, followed at a distance by copra and coconut oil. A regular island event is the arrival of a refrigerated banana ship to load cargo for Great Britain. Many thousands of stems (bunches) must be cut, trucked to the pier, and stowed in the hold in 36 hours or less.

Castries, St. Lucia's capital, sits on a big, almost landlocked harbor on the northwest coast. The town has burned down several times, most recently in 1948, leaving very little colonial architecture. Its wide main street has a center mall planted with flowering trees and is lined with squared-off structures that would be at home in Alabama. Everything shuts down for lunch from 12:30 to 1:30—except banks, which close at noon, period.

Behind Castries rises steep Morne Fortune, meaning Fortune Hill. It brought little luck to either the English or the French soldiers who, on various occasions, stormed it in the face of withering fire from entrenched defenders above. Britain took over St. Lucia by treaty in 1814, but French influence still is evident. After Castries, the main banana-loading port is Vieux Fort, the former capital, at the island's southern tip. (No one would call it Old Fort.) Country girls often wear the madras headdress normally identified with Martinique and Guadeloupe.

Sulfurous steam emerges from the bare earth of the "drive-in volcano" near Soufrière on St. Lucia. Restlessness below the surface may be noted often in the Lesser Antilles, and also may explode in violence.

168　HELLO, WEST INDIES

Near Vieux Fort is an American touch—Beane Field Airport, built by our Air Force in World War II. With another field near Castries, it gives St. Lucia two international airports. No other island in the Lesser Antilles can make that statement.

But St. Lucia's real trademark is a pair of gigantic rocks, the Pitons (PE-toNgs), on the southwest coast. They were born as volcanic necks, upwellings of molten lava. The land was much higher then. The lava solidified and stayed as the surrounding soil eroded away. Today both peaks are tree covered and rise sheer from the sea to about 2,500 feet, presenting classic landfalls for mariners and a challenge to mountain climbers.

Near the Pitons is a red-roofed village called Soufrière. It is named for a nearby crater that can be reached by road ("world's only drive-in volcano") and has bubbling-hot sulfur pools. There also are mineral springs that once were used by the French. As more tourists discover St. Lucia, they may be used again.

St. Vincent

Only 21 miles south of St. Lucia, the next Windward is smaller, poorer, more rural, but equally beautiful. Physically the two are much alike. Each is mountainous (St. Vincent's Soufrière tops 4,000 feet), well watered, and lushly green. Each has a scalloped coastline with many small bays and beaches. Each grows mainly bananas and coconuts.

St. Vincent also is the world's leading producer of arrowroot —for what that is worth. Arrowroot grows underground, like potatoes, and yields a flour which, when refined, is almost pure starch. It is used in medicines, baby food, biscuits, and puddings. It was St. Vincent's main crop until the late 1950's, when high prices for bananas led many growers to switch. Foreign users of arrowroot soon switched also—to cornstarch. St. Vincent still grows arrowroot, but finds fewer and fewer buyers.

The island capital is Kingstown, a modest city of low, red-roofed buildings on a partly sheltered harbor. It boasts a big deep-water pier, a gift of the Canadian government (which has its own foreign-aid program in the Antilles). Kingstown's three main streets are Bay, Middle, and Back. Its two main churches face

THE ENGLISH-SPEAKING WINDWARDS 169

each other across a side street. St. George's (Anglican), white and tranquil amid grass-grown burial plots, shows the simple lines of the early 1800's. St. Mary's (Catholic) displays in dark brick a welter of European cathedral styles—ornate gothic facades, romanesque courtyards, baroque towers. It was built in the 1930's under the direction of a Belgian priest working from memory, and architectural students find it arresting.

Just outside Kingstown is the oldest botanical garden in the hemisphere, founded in 1765. Among its early uses was the introduction of plants from other parts of the world to the West Indies. One of them was breadfruit, a good potential food source for island slaves. Captain William Bligh was bringing some from the Pacific on the ship *Bounty* when the famous mutiny occurred and he had to try again. In 1793 he finally landed 544 Tahitian breadfruit plants at Kingstown, and from there breadfruit was developed as a diet staple on all the islands. Today the Botanic Garden proudly exhibits an old, gnarled tree with smooth bark and waxy, dark-green leaves—a third-generation descendant of one of Bligh's cargo.

As we know, St. Vincent's volcano erupted in May 1902, one day before Mont Pelée. Soufrière had been a symmetrical crater with a clear blue lake inside, called by one observer "the most beautiful sight in the West Indies." On this day the crater destroyed the lake with flames, gases, lava, and ash. The heat seared plantations far down the mountain's slopes. Some 2,000 persons were killed. Volcanic dust helped enrich the soil of Barbados, 100 miles away. Today the lake again is beautiful, but Soufrière's upper slopes are mantled with black, lifeless ash.

From St. Vincent some 68 miles south to Grenada lie about 100 islands, cays, and rocks called the Grenadines. They are low and generally dry, but some of them once produced sugar. A dozen-odd now are inhabited by about 14,000 people, mostly poor and dependent on fishing, boatbuilding, or growing small amounts of cotton, bananas, or limes. On the northernmost island, Bequia (BECK-wee), eight miles across a deep channel from St. Vincent, a few men still practice whaling as taught their forebears by Yankees from New England, going out in homemade boats to harpoon 70-footers by hand.

Most of the Grenadines belong to St. Vincent. Grenada's jurisdiction begins 24 miles from its northern tip and includes Carriacou (Carry-a-COO), which with 13 square miles is the biggest Grenadine. Its capital, Hillsborough, is a dusty and proper village where Soviet Russian cloth is sold. Carriacou has maintained some of the tribal groupings that distinguished millions of slaves brought to the New World. Descendants of at least six African "nations"—Ibo, Mandingo, and others—remember centuries-old ways and, on special occasions, perform the ancient tribal dances.

The Grenadines' remoteness and natural beauty make them dear to yachtsmen. Charter yachts ply their waters the year round. A favorite stopping place is the Tobago Cays, a cluster of islets almost surrounded by coral reefs that offer probably the best snorkeling in the Antilles. Recently, hotels have been built on some of the islands and regular air service has been set up.

Buses load up for departure from the main square of St. George's on Grenada. They fan out all over the island, following various roads to various distances, then are turned around and driven back again.

THE ENGLISH-SPEAKING WINDWARDS   171

Grenada

Smallest of the Windwards, Grenada is the spice island of the West Indies. Though it exports cacao and bananas in quantity, its top money-making tree is the nutmeg, which yields both nutmegs—the hard kernels of the tree's pale-orange fruit—and mace, the kernel's outer covering. The mace is stripped away, dried in the sun, then ground. The remaining nut is cracked by hand and the inner "meg" removed; this is the glossy brown nutmeg of commerce.

Back in the nineteenth century, schooners sailed from Connecticut to Grenada to trade for spices. Homeward bound, a shrewd skipper with a nutmeg cargo might have his crew carve wooden ones to mix in with the real, adding up to 20 percent to the apparent total. From those days comes Connecticut's nickname, the Nutmeg State—and the cautionary phrase, "Don't take any wooden nutmegs!"

Grenada now is one of the world's leading suppliers of nutmegs and mace. It also produces cloves, cinnamon, pimento, vanilla, and black pepper, practically a whole spice shelf. The trees are placed on hillsides and flat spots all over the island, adding fragrance as well as eye appeal to the landscape. In season, the fragrance is reinforced by that of some 5,000,000 cacao trees.

Grenada's early history has a familiar ring. English colonists trying to land in 1609 were met by poisoned Carib arrows, but French settlers in 1650 were more successful. Once established, they exterminated the Indians. The last Caribs were trapped atop a sheer cliff. Refusing to surrender, they hurled their women and children into the sea and leaped after them.

English and French contested the island so vigorously that relatively few sugar planters could get established. Most of them moved away when slavery ended, leaving good land for the freed blacks. In 1843 the first nutmeg trees were brought from the East Indies, and farmers soon found them easy and profitable to raise. Grenada thus became one of the few self-supporting islands in the Antilles.

An interruption occurred in 1955, when the only hurricane in Grenada's history destroyed most of the nutmeg trees. Since those

172   HELLO, WEST INDIES

take close to 15 years to bear, many growers shifted to bananas. But nutmegs have made a good comeback, and Grenada once more could balance its budget if wages had not surged upward as well. Today Grenada gets outside aid from Great Britain, but might do better under federation with neighboring Trinidad. The idea has stirred argument on both islands.

About a third of Grenada's people live in St. George's, the capital. It has not one harbor but two. The main one is called the Carenage (pronounced French style, Ca-reh-NAZH), from its onetime service in careening ships. Next door is a basin used mainly by yachts. St. George's lies around and above both.

In the heart of town is Market Square, where fresh produce from the country is sold on Saturdays—often to people who take it right back to the country. The square also is the terminal for dozens of little buses, most of them owner-driven, painted in eye-catching colors and bearing names like "Take It Easy" or "Angel Guardian." Near by is a store called Everybody's, which advertises with the ambitious slogan, "Everybody's for Everything."

St. George's is a modern city with various churches, but many Grenadians cling to African superstitions. Some practice the rite of *shango,* which has elements reminiscent of voodoo. Drumming, dancing, and singing combine to build emotional tension in worshipers asking the aid of ancient gods. "Possession" sometimes occurs. Simulated *shango* ceremonies are offered as tourist entertainment.

Though Grenada recently has seen anti-government demonstrations by "Black Power" supporters, it remains a tourist favorite. Visitors bring more money to the island every year, a comforting thought if the market for spices should slacken.

18

BARBADOS

Farthest east of the West Indies, Barbados lies outside the main chain of the Lesser Antilles about 100 miles east of St. Vincent. Unlike its volcanic neighbors, it is composed largely of coral limestone and is nearly flat, barely topping 1,100 feet at its highest point. In outline it resembles a pork chop. Its area is only 166 square miles, so its 260,000 people (more than 95 percent black or mulatto) make it the most densely populated island in the Indies and one of the most crowded countries anywhere.

Barbados is independent within the British Commonwealth, like Jamaica and Trinidad and Tobago, with which it comprises the "Big Three" of the former British islands. A Barbadian (or Bajan, in common usage) was prime minister of the short-lived Federation of the West Indies. A campus of the University of the West Indies is just outside Bridgetown, the Bajan capital. This is a city of more than 100,000 (suburbs included) with a historic inner harbor and a new deep-water one that cost $30,000,000.

Barbados has other features. Its location makes it an airline, shipping, cable, and wireless center. (Direct jet flights bring it within four and a half hours of New York.) Four industrial parks have attracted makers of soap, clothing, mattresses, and other items. The hot but healthful climate and fine coral beaches so appeal to visitors that the island has as many hotels and guesthouses as Puerto Rico, which is more than 20 times bigger. And Barbados is a noted sugar producer, with about seven-eighths of its cultivated land in cane during some part of each year.

Lacking coal, oil, minerals, and rivers, Bajans have made the

174 HELLO, WEST INDIES

most of what they do have. Unlike many West Indians, they practice such old-fashioned virtues as hard work, thrift, and self-discipline. They believe so passionately in education that their literacy rate—better than 97 percent—is one of the highest on earth. They know what democracy means and how to keep it functioning. Obviously, they are not perfect, but they have some unusual qualities.

Bajans dress much as do their island neighbors, but speak in distinctive fashion. One local touch is emphasis on the letter *r,* which on many English-speaking islands almost disappears. A St. Vincentian, for example, makes "there" sound almost like "dey," but the Bajan word becomes "dair." Bajans often add "please" to both "yes" and "no." ("Will you have a banana?" "No, please.") To attract your attention, a Bajan may clap his hands instead of calling.

Even with hard work and thrift, the average islander has an income of only about $400 a year, higher than on most neighboring islands but low by American standards. Wages are equally low. Government clerks start at about $60 (American) a month, while canefield workers average $15 to $20 a week—when they work. Unemployment is serious, made more so by the fast population growth.

Most food is imported and relatively expensive. This is not always logical. For example, Bajans like fish. They do a lot of fishing, but mostly for flying fish. Fried, broiled, or prepared in other ways, these are so popular that Barbados sometimes is called "Land of the Flying Fish." Yet they are taken mainly in the short period from April to June. The rest of the year, nearby waters would yield dolphin, albacore, marlin, snapper, and other edible species—but the Bajans don't seem greatly interested. Instead, they eat costly imported fish.

On some islands the combination of low incomes, unemployment, and high living costs has led to serious unrest. Barbados hardly has known a disturbance in its history. One reason for this unusual record must be the history itself, which also is unusual.

It begins with the fact that Barbados was *not* discovered by Columbus. That honor apparently goes to a Portuguese captain

BARBADOS   175

who stopped by in 1536. Some say he bestowed the name Barbudos, meaning Bearded Ones, for the island's fig trees that put down aerial roots from their branches. The whole island was wooded in those days, but there was no one there, not even an Indian, when the English claimed it in 1625. Two years later they founded their first colony.

Now another fact: From 1625 until Barbados became independent in 1966, it remained wholly in British hands. Though well fortified against marauders, it was attacked only once, by Dutchmen in 1665. In the days of sail, Barbados lay too far upwind from the other Antilles for slow-moving square-riggers to take it by surprise. If they appeared, there was plenty of time to set up defenses.

English settlers streamed in and slaves soon followed. Tobacco and cotton were the first crops, but then sugarcane arrived —with predictable results. In 20 years the number of whites on the island dropped from 18,600 to 8,000, while the blacks increased from 8,300 to 50,000. Barbados became the first non-Spanish island to establish a plantocracy, and some of its aftereffects still are visible in Bajan life.

Even more marked is the impact of three centuries of unbroken British sovereignty. Barbados is the most English of the Antilles. It had its own parliament as early as 1639, and in 1652 won a guarantee to the right of self-government. The Anglican Church naturally was a strong influence. When Barbados was divided administratively into 11 parishes, ten were named for Anglican saints—James, Lucy, and so on—while the 11th became Christchurch.

Many of the original (or rebuilt) churches still are in use. At St. John's, on a hillside above the windy east coast, is a memorial to Ferdinand Paleologus, who was a vestryman there for 20 years before his death in 1679. He also was an historic figure of exotic background indeed—a direct descendant of the last Christian emperor of Byzantium (later Constantinople, now Istanbul), who was killed by a Moslem horde in 1453.

Barbados received another distinguished visitor in 1751, when a young major from North America brought his ailing half-brother to seek a health cure in the island's breeze-swept sun-

176 HELLO, WEST INDIES

shine. The cure did not occur, and the major himself contracted smallpox—but he recovered, and went on to immortality back home. His name was George Washington. In honor of this, his only trip abroad, Barbados's Beefsteak and Tripe Club holds a memorial dinner each year on or near February 22.

As the plantocracy took hold and flourished, its members gradually became able to build the fine mansions that today, in various stages of repair, are dotted about the island along with old churches and wind-driven sugar mills. From slavery days also dates the distinctive Bajan dwelling, originally called a chattel house. In essence this is a tiny two-room wooden rectangle, about eight feet by 16 feet, with a steeply peaked roof. Narrow double doors, slatted to let in air, are hung in the center of one long wall. Above them are little transom windows. Other windows with slatted shutters are on either side of the doors and at the ends of the house. Coral-block front steps are common. Many householders add wooden trim along the eaves, a doorstep-sized porch, or a full porch the length of the house.

The whole thing is easy and cheap to build, repair, or take down to move to another location. If the family needs more space, the owner cuts a doorway in the other long wall and builds an identical house against it. In time he may have two or three such annexes, each with its own peaked roof. These dwellings are almost as small and "busy" with detail as a child's playhouse, but they are truly Bajan. Even well-to-do families with larger homes favor the double doors and the slats for ventilation.

For contrast there are the island's hotels. These form two main groups along the southern and western coasts, with Bridgetown in between. The south-coast hotels range from fairly expensive to quite inexpensive, and include plain, prim guesthouses that would look at home in English seaside resorts. They are strung along the narrow coastal road, interspersed with scores of middle-class homes of the type the English call villas. Sometimes it takes a horse-drawn cart, or a man riding a donkey, to remind the visitor that he still is in the tropics.

The west-coast hotels are generally more exclusive and priced accordingly. They run to larger grounds, swimming pools, big staffs, and other Caribbean features. Their area is known, not without cause, as the Platinum Coast.

Barbadian harbor police use a row boat to patrol the narrow waters of Bridgetown's Careenage. Their uniforms, much like those once worn by Admiral Nelson's sailors, bespeak Bajan regard for things British.

As for Bridgetown, it began as a settlement by a stream and grew into a port around a long, narrow inlet still called the Careenage (pronounced Coreenage, in contrast with Carenage, Grenada's main harbor). Its Englishness was only faintly modified by immigration from Scotland and Ireland, plus a few Jewish refugees from South America. As sugar profits multiplied, Bridgetown merchants prospered accordingly. After Admiral Sir Horatio Nelson was killed at the Battle of Trafalgar, they named a dockside area Trafalgar Square and had a monument to Nelson erected there —both ahead of London. The Harbor Police still wear bell-bottomed trousers with long-sleeved white jerkins and straw hats, the uniform of Nelson's sailors.

Bridgetown contains one of the older Anglican cathedrals, St. Michael's, where birds flit through open windows and lizards scurry along the stone walls during sermons. But the capital is not wedded to the past. Modern stores, a drive-in theater, and big suburban housing developments are strictly of today. So are the traffic snarls and the hurrying pedestrians along Broad Street. British weights and measures are used, but Barbados has its own currency (the East Caribbean dollar) and government savings banks. Of Bridgetown's five commercial banks, one is English, one American, and three are Canadian. There are good

Children play outside a typical Bajan house. It shows the design features common to thousands of these little homes, from the peaked roof and double doors to the louvers for air in doors and shutters.

BARBADOS 179

restaurants and colorful night spots. The Queen Elizabeth Hospital, opened in 1964, has 600 beds and is one of the best in the West Indies. With other hospitals, infirmaries, and health centers, it gives Bajans a high level of medical care.

Outside Bridgetown, the island is likely to strike the visitor as a solid sea of sugarcane. Some 800 miles of paved roads make travel easy, but when the cane is ripe the average road almost disappears between tall, pale-green walls. The adventure of driving the winding, English-style lanes is increased by such English-style directional signs as "Pie Corner via Graveyard." Bajans generally greet one another along the roads and extend this courtesy to visitors, with guidance if needed.

Barbados rises northeastward from Bridgetown, through the cane. The east coast, locally called Scotland, is surprisingly wild and rugged. Rocky headlands stand between beaches where long rollers meet their first obstacle since leaving Africa. Bajans themselves prefer this coast for vacations. Near the village of Bathsheba is the base of the flying-fish fleet, which at the height of the season includes scores of powered craft. In the morning they race one another 25 miles or so to offshore banks, and in the afternoon they race back again. Some of the catch is frozen and shipped to England, but most is sold locally. Housewives respond to the cry "Fish hey!" because in Barbados "fish" has to mean flying fish.

On the east coast also is a low, moss-covered stone building approached by a driveway between towering royal palms and ponds choked with water plants. This is the entrance to Codrington College, opened in 1745 with funds willed for the purpose by Charles Codrington, governor of the Leeward Islands. (He succeeded his father in that post, and like his father was sole owner of Barbuda.) Codrington was the first theological seminary in the West Indies, and, after some years of association with England's Durham University, it again functions as one today.

Overall, the Bajan concern for education contrasts with that of most other island governments. About 20 percent of the national budget goes for education. There are about 140 public schools, primary and secondary, and about 50 private ones. The government pays tuition fees for students at the local university campus

180   HELLO, WEST INDIES

—which enrolls more than 400 students and is noted for its agricultural courses—and gives some scholarships for study abroad. There are technical and vocational schools. A long-established teachers' college draws students from other islands. Bajans may receive specialized instruction in such advanced techniques as guidance counseling and teaching handicapped children.

The government also has furthered Bajan sports by hiring coaches, building facilities, and encouraging promising youngsters. Cricket, understandably, is the national game. Barbados produces more than its share of good players and tends to dominate the selections for the international West Indies team. Bajans also can engage in soccer, athletics, basketball, tennis—or, in many parts of the island, step across the road and go swimming.

In recent years Barbados has been the site of several international scientific projects. Canada's McGill University has done studies of marine biology, water desalting, and high-altitude conditions for space probes. (The last has sent test missiles as high as 85 miles.) A six-year United Nations study of Caribbean deep-sea fishing resources has had its main base on Barbados. The island joined the United States government in the Barbados Oceanographic and Meteorological Experiment. This is the largest single effort ever made to learn more about the earth's oceans and its atmosphere, involving scores of separate projects.

Such things, unfortunately, create few jobs—and jobs remain the Bajans' top need. Tourism probably cannot be expanded a great deal farther. Most factories are small, and new ones come slowly. The problem is underlined by the gradually falling world price of sugar. To lower production costs, the Bajans have experimented with machinery to harvest and handle the cane. But such machinery would throw still more men out of work.

As on many other islands, some of the best-educated young people have solved their personal employment problem by emigrating. But most have stayed. They are part of an unusual nation. Despite their almost excessive Englishness, the Bajans have taken full responsibility for their own future. Few are attracted by "Black Power." Instead, they point to the motto on the national coat of arms: "Pride and Industry." These could be just old-fashioned words, but the Bajans seem to mean them.

19

TRINIDAD AND TOBAGO

The two most southerly islands of the Lesser Antilles chain make up one country. Trinidad and Tobago (T. and T.) has natural beauty, substantial resources, unusual history, and a unique mixture of races. It is noted for lovely women. It gave the world the steel band, calypso music, limbo dancing, and an annual Carnival without equal. It is lively and often happy. It also has problems.

The two islands lie off the northern mouths of Venezuela's great Orinoco River, some 2,000 miles southeast of New York. Physically, they could hardly be more different. Trinidad covers 1,864 square miles; Tobago, only 116. (Their combined area is about four-fifths that of Delaware.) Trinidad has over a million people; Tobago, about 35,000. Trinidad has a northern range of steep mountains topping 3,000 feet, other hills to east and south, and a flat center. All of Tobago is a single ridge no more than 1,850 feet high.

Trinidad has big oil refineries, growing industry, and extensive agriculture. Tobago exports almost nothing but coconuts—but outdraws its relatively huge neighbor in tourist appeal with Buccoo Reef (snorkeling in waist-deep water), Bird of Paradise Island (the only wild birds of paradise in the hemisphere, brought from New Guinea in 1909), and the tantalizing question: Was Tobago the original setting for *Robinson Crusoe?*

Trinidad is cosmopolitan and colorful, a Caribbean crossroads with a largely peaceful past. Tobago is a rural outpost 20 miles northeast, yet in its day was one of the most sought-after prizes in the Caribbean. The islands first were joined in 1889 as a con-

182 HELLO, WEST INDIES

venience for the British Colonial Office. In 1962 they became the second independent West Indian nation (25 days after Jamaica) within the Commonwealth. Port of Spain on Trinidad is the capital and chief city (population 100,000-plus), but Tobago also has a capital, Scarborough (population about 4,000).

Geologically, Trinidad was part of South America until quite recently. Its northern mountains continue those in Venezuela that project east to form Paria Peninsula. The mountains nourish forests of flowering trees and such animals as the agouti, alligator, armadillo, and wild hog. The local name for the last is *quenk,* which seems just right for a hog.

Mainland birds also are numerous on the island. There is the friendly little keskidee, whose name renders phonetically the French phrase *"Qu'est-ce qui dit?"*—"Who says?" The keskidee repeats the question all day long, but never waits for an answer. The rare scarlet ibis, a wading bird of brilliant red plumage, breeds in Caroni Swamp, protected by the government. But the island's particular pride is its 18 species of hummingbird. The Indians who occupied Trinidad when Columbus came by in 1498 apparently called it Iere (YEH-ray), meaning Land of the Hummingbird.

Trinidad is roughly rectangular, with peninsulas at the northwest and southwest corners. The northern one is extended by islands to just seven miles from Venezuela; the passages between are called the Dragon's Mouths. The southern peninsula leaves a wider gap, the Serpent's Mouth. The southern peninsula is Trinidad's oil zone. Though its known reserves are dwindling, it yields some 50 million barrels a year, and drilling has begun on extensive new offshore oil and gas fields. Meanwhile, Venezuela supplies another 80 million barrels of crude a year. Practically all the oil is refined near the port of San Fernando, Trinidad's second city. Oil is T. and T.'s main export by far and brings the average annual income to about $600, highest of any independent Antillean country.

Behind oil in value come natural gas, and asphalt from famous Pitch Lake. Also on the southern peninsula, this is the largest asphalt deposit on earth, covering some 90 acres. Theories on its origin differ, but the asphalt is basically thick crude oil mixed

TRINIDAD AND TOBAGO   183

with earth. When some is dug from the lake, the hole soon refills. Sir Walter Raleigh, among others, used the asphalt to calk ships' planking. Commercial exploitation, mainly for roads in the United States and Europe, began in 1888. By now it is estimated that 13 million tons have been removed, with 45 million to go.

Traditionally Trinidad was a sugar island, and that still is its main crop (followed by cacao, citrus, and copra). It produced little of anything, though, for nearly three centuries after Columbus. The first permanent Spanish community, San José (now St. Joseph, east of Port of Spain) was not founded until 1584. Few settlers followed, and they did not prosper. There were only 300 slaves on the island in 1783 when the Crown finally opened it to foreign colonization. Frenchmen from Haiti and other islands then came to plant sugarcane. The number of slaves increased. But the island still was so lightly settled that an English force captured it easily in 1797. Five years later it became English by treaty.

The new owners did not have time to import a great many slaves before emancipation in 1834. Blacks on Trinidad and Tobago then numbered about 26,500, fewer than on many smaller islands. After emancipation the white landowners sought other farmhands. Chinese and Portuguese came, but soon took up commercial pursuits. Then, over a period of 70 years, the British government underwrote the importation of nearly 150,000 indentured workers from India. Some went home when their contract period was up, but many were offered land and stayed. They became shopkeepers as well as farmers, forming virtually all-Indian villages where domed Hindu temples or the slim minarets of Moslem mosques replaced the spires of Christian churches. More Moslems came later from the Middle East, particularly Syria and Lebanon.

Today the population is classified as about 43 percent of African origin, 36 percent Indian, 16 percent "mixed," three percent European, and two percent Chinese. Trinidad has been called a miniature United Nations.

Tobago by contrast never had many immigrants from anywhere, yet was involved in much more warfare than Trinidad. Apparently sighted and christened by Columbus, it sat quietly

184 HELLO, WEST INDIES

until the 1600's. Then its usefulness as a naval base attracted not only England, France, and Holland, but also, of all places, the Baltic principality of Courland (later Latvia, now part of the Soviet Union).* So much fighting went on over Tobago that in 1704 it was declared neutral ground. Sixty years later the English seized the island, then lost it to the French, regained it, lost it again, and finally took firm control in 1803.

Slavery ended without incident and most former slaves turned to sugar planting. In 1884 the sugar market collapsed. Five years later, with Tobago practically starving, Britain joined it to Trinidad. People on both islands objected, but today most not only have accepted their status but also are proud of it.

Trinidad's many immigrants have left many traces. Little native Indian blood remains, though such place names as Caroni and Arima predate Columbus. Spanish place names are more numerous, and Spanish still is spoken in some mountain villages. From Venezuela come *aguinaldos,* carols occasionally heard at Christmas.

French influence is stronger still. Again there are place names (including the graphic Morne Mal d'Estomac, Mount Stomach Ache), and many people speak a Créole patois similar to that of the Windward Islands. French folk dances still are popular. The rousing Carnival now regarded as "typically West Indian" actually began with French planters who held a season of parties and masked balls between Christmas and Lent. Slaves were excluded, but eagerly took over and enlarged on the idea after emancipation.

The African element, of course, dominates in T. and T. It may appear in folk beliefs and pastimes—such as limbo dancing, which has evolved from rural amusement to professional show. A stunt as much as a dance, limbo requires the performer to ease

Hindu temples are a common sight on Trinidad. This one has typical roof and entrance design, with candles burning inside the doorway under paintings of Hindu gods. On the steps is a turbaned priest.

* The only Latvian mementos on Tobago are names: Courland Point and adjoining Great Courland Bay.

186 HELLO, WEST INDIES

under a low horizontal bar, in step with a drumbeat, knees bent until his body is parallel to the floor, but never touching. Some dancers manage this under a bar only eight inches from the floor.

Many Trinidadians still take some stock in such old African figures as Papa Bois, god of the woods, Maman de l'Eau, goddess of the waters, the witch La Diablesse, the werewolf Louahou (Loup Garou), and others whose names, incidentally, all are French. There is *shango* on Trinidad, as on Grenada, and illegal *obeah,* but apparently no voodoo. In any case there always is a big and colorful turnout for church on Sunday.

The super-turnout is for Carnival, just before Lent begins. Carnival proper lasts only two days on Trinidad, but preparations begin almost a year ahead. Individuals and groups decide how they will get themselves up—as historic figures, bats, devils, pirates, spacemen, or any of dozens of other things—and some groups detail a member to research authentic costumes. These may cost $500 or more apiece (almost a year's earnings for some) and involve taste, inventiveness, and a lot of work. Meanwhile steel bands begin rehearsing music written just for Carnival. So do calypso singers. Starting in January, singers and musicians perform all over the island. During Carnival valuable prizes are awarded for notable costumes, outstanding steel bands, the Calypso King, and so on.

All the preparation paves the way for Carnival's real purpose: providing a high old time for everyone. "Jump-ups" (group dancing) are almost continuous in the streets, dance halls, and clubs. Bands of up to 2,000 persons, costumed alike, march in joyful tempo through Port of Spain. Rum is consumed in gargantuan amounts. Everyone likes everyone. Tourists come by thousands to watch, and usually end by joining in. It all stops at midnight before Ash Wednesday, then starts again for next year.

And then there are the Indian get-togethers. Each year the Moslem festival of Hosein (pronounced Ho-say) is celebrated all over Trinidad. It honors two brothers, Hosein and Hassan, who were killed by treachery in a holy war. Processions are held for several days. They feature huge decorative constructions called *tadjahs*—made of bamboo, colored paper, tinsel, and glass to resemble ornate mosques—which are drawn through the streets

TRINIDAD AND TOBAGO   187

on carts. Thousands of persons of Indian descent, Hindu as well as Moslem, march along chanting songs to the memory of the murdered brothers. Drummers (often Negro) pound on Indian drums, and stick-fighters battle with wooden staves. The climax comes when the procession reaches a river or the sea and the *tadjahs* are cast into the water.

The Hindus have their own annual event, the Diwali or festival of lights. Its purification rites once were held in India's sacred Ganges River, but on Trinidad the worshipers use Manzanilla Beach, across the island from Port of Spain. Another Hindu custom is to place red, white, or green flags on bamboo poles in the yard of one's home (preferably near a mango tree) as a thanks offering to Hanuman, the Monkey God, for help on a family problem—restoring the father's health, say, or finding a son a job. Each flag-raising usually calls for a party to which friends and neighbors, Hindu or not, are invited.

Overall, there is increasing contact among the various groups on Trinidad, though the two main ones, African and Indian, have mixed feelings toward each other. The blacks who left the estates after emancipation looked down on the Indians who replaced them. The Indians returned the compliment. Today they tend to split over politics. Most blacks support the People's National Movement of Dr. Eric Williams, which took power when T. and T. became independent. The opposition Democratic Labor Party attracts the Indians. Since the Indians are increasing at a faster rate than the blacks, the DLP one day should become the majority party.

The two-party system is one of many things bequeathed to the country by the English. Their most visible monument is Port of Spain. Set on the coast where central flatland meets northern mountains, it looks west toward Venezuela. The waterfront and downtown area are generally modern and bustling, with several tall new buildings. Restaurants large and small offer food reflecting Trinidad's many backgrounds, from Venezuelan *arepas* (turnovers) and Indian *roti* (smaller turnovers) to African stews, Chinese specialties, and French cuisine.

Here also is sprawling Red House, seat of the island government. Built in 1906 in true British colonial style, it rambles over

188 HELLO, WEST INDIES

most of two blocks. Before it is a park where anyone can make a speech, put on an impromptu dance, buy a snack from a pushcart, or just sit and watch. With fewer tropical trees and dark skins, it might be Hyde Park in London.

Port of Spain's main park is the Savannah, generally called Queen's Park. (The queen was Victoria.) Once a sugar estate, it covers some 380 acres—enough for a racetrack, a bandstand, trees, walks, and a dozen cricket matches at the same time. Fronting on this expanse are some of the most astonishing nineteenth-century "gingerbread" mansions ever built, rich with gables, turrets, pinnacles, bay windows, and jigsaw ornamentation. One reportedly was modeled on a German castle. Another was built for the visit of a titled Rumanian, who never showed up. Some now are empty, but one of the most ornate is used as the prime minister's office.

The capital also has its slums. They developed, as elsewhere, largely from the immigration of poor, unskilled country people. They knew a period of relative prosperity during World War II, when an American military area was set up on the peninsula a few miles northwest. The presence of soldiers, sailors, and airmen created a demand for various services. "Workin' for the Yankee dollah" became a way of life. But the Yankees began leaving after the war, and the area reverted to T. and T. in 1967.*

The early postwar years saw many slum dwellers out of work again, particularly young men and teenagers. Uninterested in school, they often joined gangs and wound up involved in stealing and fighting. (Drugs had not appeared on the scene then, but have since.) A virtual state of war developed between the gangs and the police.

It was then, in the late 1940's, that Trinidad's famous steel band was born. It grew out of the island-wide fascination with drums. For many years they had been part of everything from casual street parades to Carnival festivities. Almost every culture contributed—big African drums, smaller Indian ones, maracas from Spanish lands. The French word for drum, *tambour,* got

---

* It had been leased for 99 years, so the Americans left 73 years early. Before doing so, they built some highways that still are among Trinidad's best. One snakes over the northern mountains to bring the outstanding beach at Maracas Bay within a half hour of Port of Spain.

TRINIDAD AND TOBAGO 189

into the picture when sections of bamboo trunk were used as drums and called bamboo-tamboos. ("Tamboo" here is the same as the *tambú* of Curaçao.)

Young slum dwellers drummed on anything, including odd bits of metal: cracker tins, trash-can covers, scrap iron. Then someone discovered that the end of a steel oil drum produced a pleasant sound, and that different notes could result from hitting it in different spots. Cut away from the rest of the oil drum, the "pan" could be handled like a conventional drum but with a mellow, resonant tone when struck with rubber-tipped sticks. Some "pan beaters" became expert tuners, making each note exact by heating the steel surface and hammering it to the proper tension. Gradually three main sizes of drum evolved: Ping Pongs, on which the melody of a tune is played; Tune Booms, for the harmony notes; Booms, for bass notes. Few drummers to this day can read music.

The first steel bands in Port of Spain outraged citizens who saw them as one more obnoxious slum product. Police were encouraged to break them up. But slowly it appeared that the bands were giving a sense of purpose to their performers. Gang rivalries began to be expressed in drum competition rather than with knives. When the "pan beaters" formed permanent practice areas, the government quietly supplied funds to help make them into neighborhood centers. Their activities now include parties, sports, and even vocational-training courses. Trinidad still has juvenile delinquency but, says one official, "The steel band has saved our island from gang warfare." And each year at Carnival time, bandsmen march to police headquarters, the onetime enemy camp, to serenade officers whose duties keep them away from the celebration.

Steel bands have spread all over the Caribbean. So has calypso. This basically is a type of song. The music is simple and repetitive, but the words are something special. Humorous, sly, mocking, they comment on just about anything—politics and race relations, headlined crimes and catastrophes, public personalities and the more private contest of Man vs. Woman. Calypso grew out of folk song. Since the 1930's it has been the province of inventive entertainers with such wondrous names as Lord Executor, Atilla the Hun, and Mighty Sparrow.

Meanwhile, in and out of the slums, T. and T. fights unem-

Segments of oil drums make the instruments of a Trinidadian steel band. Biggest "pans" produce deepest notes. Steel bands have kept many teenagers from what used to be a favorite pastime: gang wars.

ployment. Oil brings in money, but the refineries require relatively few workers. Agriculture needs them, but many country dwellers drift to the cities and lack the skills for modern farming or much of anything else. The government thus has embarked on a long-range program to improve education and attract industry.

Enough schools have been built so that free education now is available through ninth grade. (Formerly, only those who passed a stiff exam could expect it beyond sixth grade.) Past ninth grade

TRINIDAD AND TOBAGO   191

there are academic and trade schools, and three government institutes for technical and vocational training. The Trinidad campus of the University of the West Indies offers liberal arts but emphasizes agriculture and engineering.

Too many youngsters still drop out of school, particularly after sixth grade. Some industries run trade schools and apprentice programs for children of their employees. Recently the government added a program of youth camps where dropouts can learn basic skills. Each boy is fed, housed, and given a small weekly allowance for up to two years. Thousands have taken this training with generally good results. Other West Indian governments are watching interestedly.

As for industry, T. and T. favors factories that need a lot of workers, such as makers of clothing, packers of vegetables and fruits, and assemblers of radios. A growing number of such plants operate in Trinidad City, between Port of Spain and the international airport. This is a carefully planned development with through highways for heavy traffic, local feeder roads, residential areas, air-conditioned factories, and other modern features.

T. and T. shares with other islands the "brain drain" of those who can better themselves elsewhere. Some well-known native sons live abroad for personal reasons, including novelist V. S. Naipaul, singer Harry Belafonte, and black militant Stokely Carmichael. But others have stayed home, among them poet-playwright Derek Walcott (whose *Dream on Monkey Mountain* has been produced on the New York stage and on American television), novelist Samuel Selvon, and most of the best local artists—the creators of prize-winning Carnival costumes.

Emigration takes some pressure off the labor market, but unemployment still runs as high as 25 percent. This was the underlying reason for the riots in Trinidad in spring 1970.

The immediate trigger was a $33,000 fine imposed on ten Trinidadian students at a Montreal university after they wrecked a million-dollar computer center to protest alleged discrimination against blacks. The T. and T. government paid the fine. But island militants, angry over joblessness and the racial attitudes they tended to blame it on, began a series of strikes. Then part of the 720-man army mutinied. Crowds gathered even on placid

192 HELLO, WEST INDIES

Tobago, where whites driving the country roads received clenched-fist salutes and shouts of "Powah!"—often accompanied by smiles, as though it were a kind of game. But on Trinidad the game was serious, with rioting, looting, and shooting. It ended only when Prime Minister Williams declared a state of emergency, quelled the army mutiny, and restored peace in the streets—until next time.

That there would be other such times seemed inevitable. Whites still owned some of the best land, factories, stores, and hotels. Blacks still wanted work, some desperately. "Black Power" might not be the answer, but Trinidad and Tobago had to find one.

20

HELP!

The islands of the West Indies share one overriding concern: to make a better way of life for their people—fast.

In preceding chapters we have seen the main reasons for the concern. They include too many people, too few jobs, too few schools, poor housing, poor nutrition, racial unrest. We have looked at some causes: lack of natural resources, exploitation by colonial powers, the aftereffects of slavery, continuing dependence on one or two crops, political instability. Similar conditions exist in other areas where people only recently have been given self-government—with similar results. How all the developing nations meet their many problems is extremely important to the rest of the world.

The West Indies start with some things in their favor. They have sunshine, beaches, and other appealing physical aspects. They are near enough to North America to attract tourists by the millions. Most islanders identify democracy with material progress and want to move ahead under that system. (Cuba and Haiti may or may not be permanent exceptions.) Race relations generally are better than in, say, the United States.

But the islands are poor, in some cases appallingly so. Life might be better if the Antilles could be sealed off and people had a simple, happy Arawak existence. But now is now. The islanders know what people in more developed countries have—nice houses, cars, TV sets, schools, paid vacations, and all the rest— and want the same for themselves. That means money, and money means jobs. With minor exceptions, there are not enough any-

194 HELLO, WEST INDIES

where. Developing more is what plagues island leaders, particularly because it takes so much time and people don't want to wait.

In these conditions every island has had to look outside for help. The response ranges from charity to hard-headed business, usually in one of four categories:

Government gifts, such as the British and French subsidies to island sugar growers, the Soviet handouts to Cuba, or the American aid to the Dominican Republic.

Private investments by foreigners, as in the oil refineries on Puerto Rico, Curaçao, and Trinidad, the bauxite mines on Jamaica, or most resort hotels.

Loans to island businessmen, such as an importer on St. Maarten or a planter on Barbados.

Tourist spending at hotels, restaurants, places of amusement, and shops, with the money quickly respent for local wages, food, taxes, and so on.

Except for the outright gifts, all such help comes at a price. The investors create jobs and boost government revenues, but take their profits away. The lenders of money expect to be repaid, with interest. The tourists demand accommodations, food, diversion, and service (and much of their outlay goes to buy imported goods). The islanders pay the price or lose the help.

In any case, all these things are only temporary in terms of the long-range cry for industry and jobs. Almost every island is trying frantically to lure or set up factories, meanwhile building tourism. The effort is not made easier by the fact that practically all the islands are competing with one another. They compete for markets, for tourists, and even for industry. When one needy island lands a new plant, it often means that an equally needy island tried to land it and failed.

Why don't the islands stop competing and get together?

On the surface there is no convincing reason. The fact that some islands are independent and others tied to foreign governments is a complication, but not necessarily fatal. Differences in geography and language hardly are greater than in Europe, where the European Economic Community—the Common Market—has benefited all concerned. The existence of the Common Market actually makes island cooperation more urgent,

HELP! 195

for Britain's entry into the EEC (which is reported almost certain as this is written) will mean an end, sooner or later, to the way London has been supporting Commonwealth sugar production. Any new arrangement requiring the approval of all EEC members may be much less favorable to the growers. That would impose severe economic strains on all the former British islands. In sheer self-interest they would have to find methods of working together.

Up to now, though, most islanders have resisted mutual action that might help someone else at their expense. We have seen how the Federation of the West Indies, which must have looked very good on paper, failed when one island got out rather than take chances. Other proposals for federation come up now and then. Few listen.

Some cooperative steps have been taken. Every island government except Cuba has a board to promote tourism, and most of them belong to the Caribbean Travel Association. This maintains a New York City office and puts out information designed to interest Americans in the islands as a group. The University of the West Indies is a bond among English-speaking islands. So is CARIFTA (the Caribbean Free Trade Association), established in 1968 with the aim of increasing trade among former British islands. The first step was a gradual reduction in mutual tariffs on copra, fruit, tobacco, and biscuits. How much good this will do is uncertain. The main markets for most island products are industrial nations, not other islands.

Perhaps more valuable are two agencies designed to aid the West Indies as a whole. First is the Caribbean Economic Development Corporation (1966), organized by Puerto Rico to stimulate trade, and the exchange of ideas and technical help, throughout the area. Second is the Caribbean Development Bank (1968), set up mainly to lend money in any independent island except Cuba, using funds from the United States, Canada, Great Britain, and Puerto Rico.

Signs of high-level cooperation, however, may not impress the man in the street. On most islands he is likely to be told that his government really is the tool of foreign capitalists and that he is being exploited by foreigners and/or whites. The governments should be replaced. The foreigners should be thrown out. The

196 HELLO, WEST INDIES

refineries, mines, hotels, and so on should be taken over. Such thinking is encouraged by propaganda from Cuba, Russia, and Red China. It appeals to some impoverished islanders who feel they cannot wait for things to improve by themselves.

On former British islands, advocates of "Black Power" say that social change depends on racial progress. They cite the thinking of Jamaica's Marcus Garvey—or Trinidad's Stokely Carmichael. Even on black islands, they say, whites still dominate. They sneer at mulatto government leaders who, according to one militant, "run the plantation for whites and fail to use political power for the good of their people." The remedy presumably would be to seize the power and put it to better use.

This thinking also has appeal, though it is opposed by many. Opponents say no island can develop even the jobs it needs, much less social justice for all, without outside capital—white men's money. And whites clearly are unlikely to risk money where a government's stated policy is "Out with the whites!"

Some "Black Power" supporters admit the financial problem. Some brush it aside. Some say in effect, "Don't worry. We'll get money. There are whites who will let us have it on our terms. There are nonwhites we can call on. There is Russia. And Red China. . . ."

So the argument goes on, breaking out now and then in the kind of violence that scarred Trinidad and Tobago, and later Grenada, in 1970. "Black Power" proponents hope to create more violence. Island governments hope to be able to repress it. The argument is far from over.

Meanwhile, the biggest single factor in the future of the West Indies may be the United States. This is less because of government policy than because ours is a rich nation and the Antilles are close.

Consider tourism. Though the islands attract Europeans, Latin Americans, and Canadians, above all they draw Americans. The Yankee dollar comes in larger numbers every year, and more and more islanders work for it. On some islands it already spells the difference between prosperity and near disaster.

Consider American products. From cars to cola drinks, they are sold on virtually every island and often preferred to compet-

Here is one expression of West Indian tensions: the American ambassador's car burns in the 1962 civil war in the Dominican Republic. But the country still has problems, and still needs American help.

ing products from other countries. With them come American techniques in display, advertising, even use. The island housewife who bypasses salt cod in the outdoor market for frozen veal in a supermarket has cast an unconscious vote for the American way of life.

Consider American movies, radio, television, magazines, books. Their impact is huge. They give a picture of the United States that, though often distorted or out of focus, normally fascinates most foreigners. West Indians are no exception. Most of them look on us as the leader of the world's free nations. Hundreds of thousands have emigrated to our "land of opportunity," while those

198   HELLO, WEST INDIES

who stay home follow many of our styles in clothing, home decoration, cultural activities, amusements, even politics.

Not every islander admires us, to be sure. We are criticized on many grounds, from our policies in Southeast Asia to race relations at home, from the brassiness of some American tourists to the complaint that others spend too little, and so on through a long catalog of real and not-so-real grievances. On a few islands we are officially hated. On others we are regarded as—well, at least not so bad as the British or the French or whoever it may be.

Yet there are many who dream of solving their problems by joining the United States. If Hawaii could become a state, they think, why not Hispaniola or Barbados? Few island leaders would admit such thoughts publicly. They are proud of their beautiful little countries, hopeful for the future, eager to show how well they can meet all problems.

The fact remains: Every island needs outside help. There are Canada, Great Britain, France, the Netherlands, the Soviet Union, the United Nations. But nearest, richest, and most concerned is the United States.

200 HELLO, WEST INDIES

RECOMMENDED READING

Among the printed sources consulted in preparing this book, the following are recommended for further reading (alphabetically within sections):

- **Early history**

  Carse, Robert. *The Age of Piracy*. New York: Rinehart & Co., Inc., 1957. Fast-moving, simply written review of how the best-known pirates of the Spanish Main got that way.

  Morison, Samuel. *Admiral of the Ocean Sea*. Boston: Little, Brown & Co., 1942. Outstanding among the many accounts of Columbus's discovery of the New World.

- **The area today**

  Leigh Fermor, Patrick. *The Traveller's Tree*. New York: Harper & Row, 1951. A minor classic by a young Englishman who wandered the eastern Caribbean before the tourist rush began and set down many perceptive observations on people, places, and customs.

  Mitchell, Carleton. *Isles of the Caribbees*. Washington, D.C.: National Geographic Society, 1966. Nonpolitical information on most of the Lesser Antilles, much of it first published in the National Geographic magazine.

  Rodman, Selden. *The Caribbean*. New York: Hawthorn Books, Inc., 1968. Personal impressions of the whole area, including interviews with many island personalities.

  Slater, Mary. *The Caribbean Islands*. New York: The Viking Press, 1968. An intelligent Englishwoman's view of the region.

- **By islands**

  Cargill, Morris, ed. *Ian Fleming Introduces Jamaica*. New York: Hawthorn Books, Inc., 1965. Essays by Jamaican writers on aspects of the island from history and folklore to skin diving and stamp collecting.

  Craton, Michael. *A History of the Bahamas*. London: Collins, 1969. The text used in most Bahamian schools.

  Fergusson, Erna. *Cuba*. New York: Alfred A. Knopf, 1946.

RECOMMENDED READING 201

Good readable description of the island and its people B. C. —Before Castro.

Lewis, Gordon K. *Puerto Rico: Freedom and Power in the Caribbean*. New York: The Monthly Review Press, 1963. Thorough, thoughtful examination of life in Puerto Rico and the effects of American dominion on the island's people.

Martin, John Bartlow. *Overtaken by Events*. Garden City, N.Y.: Doubleday & Co., Inc., 1966. Detailed account of the 1965–66 Dominican civil war, by the then American ambassador there.

Rodman, Selden. *Haiti, the Black Republic*. New York; Devin Adair Co., 1961. Sympathetic report on Haiti, its people, their history, and their art.

―――. *Quisqueya*. Seattle: University of Washington Press, 1964. Probably the best history in English of the Dominican Republic up to the early 1960's.

INDEX

Agriculture, 3, 5, 11, 16–17, 48.
  See also Sugarcane
American Virgin Islands, *see* U.S.
  Virgin Islands
Andros, 59
Anegada, 131
Anguilla, 143, 148
Antigua, 143, 149–51
Antilles
  islands comprising, 3
  origin of name, 2
  see also specific islands
Arawak Indians, 2, 28–30, 31, 34,
  59, 107–08, 137
Architecture, 14–16, 17, 33
  Citadelle Laferrière, 97–98
  haciendas, 46–47, 50
  Sans Souci palace, 97
  see also specific cities
Aristocracy, *see* Plantocracy
Art
  Cuba, 70
  Dominican Republic, 107
  Haiti, 93–95
  Puerto Rico, 121
Aruba, 132, 136–37. *See also*
  Netherlands Antilles
Associated States, British, 143, 163.
  See also specific islands

Bahama Islands
  climate, 54
  economy, 61–63
  education, 55
  ethnic composition, 55
  geography, 3, 6, 54–55, 58
  government, 3, 55
  history, 1–2, 59–61
  motto, 59
  Nassau, 56, 59
  Out Islands, 56–59
  population, 56
  tourism, 54, 58, 61–62
Bajans, *see* Barbados
Balaguer, Joaquín, 112
Barbados

Bridgetown, 173, 177–79
  economy, 173, 174, 180
  education, 17–18, 174, 179–80
  English influence, 175, 177
  ethnic composition, 173, 175
  food specialties, 174
  geography, 173, 179
  government, 173, 174
  history, 174–76
  language, 174
  population, 173
  religion, 175
  sports, 180
  tourism, 176
Barbuda, 150
Basse Terre (city, Guadeloupe),
  159
Basse Terre (island), 157, 158
Basseterre (St. Kitts), 144–45
Batista, Fulgencio, 70–71, 72
Bequia, 169
Bimini, 59
Bird of Paradise Island, 181
Birthrates, 5
Black magic, 26
"Black Power" movements, 5, 196
  Grenada, 172
  Jamaica, 83
  Trinidad and Tobago, 187, 191–
    92
  U.S. Virgin Islands, 129
Bobadilla, Francisco, 33
Bogle, Paul, 81
Bonaire, 132, 137. *See also* Nether-
  lands Antilles
Bosch, Juan, 110–12
Bradshaw, Robert, 144
Brethren of the Coast, 42, 96
Bridgetown (Barbados), 173, 177–
  79
Brimston Hill (St. Kitts), 146
British Associated States, 143, 163.
  See also specific islands
British Virgin Islands, 130–31
Bustamante, Alexander, 83

203

204   HELLO, WEST INDIES

Caicos and Turks Islands, 63
Calenda, 22–23
Calypso, 189
Carib Indians, 2, 29–30, 36
  Dominica reservation, 164, 165–66
  Grenada extermination, 171
  St. Kitts massacre, 146
Caribbean, origin of name, 2
Caribbean Development Bank, 195
Caribbean Economic Development Corporation, 195
Caribbean Free Trade Association (CARIFTA), 195
Carnival
  Antigua, 151
  Curaçao, 136
  Guadeloupe, 157
  Martinique, 157
  Trinidad, 181, 184, 186
  Windward Islands (English-speaking), 164
Carriacou, 170
Castries (St. Lucia), 166
Castro, Fidel, 4, 71–77
Cat Island, 58
Cayman Islands, 88
Charlotte Amalie (St. Thomas), 125–26, 127
Christianity, influence of, 24–25
Christophe, Henri, 97–98
Citadelle Laferrière, 97–98
Climate, 4–5, 6, 8–9
  influence of, 10–11
  see also specific islands
Codrington, Charles, 179
Codrington, Christopher, 150
Colonization, 30–36, 37–38, 42–45
Columbus, Bartolomé, 103–4
Columbus, Christopher, 1–2, 9, 30–34, 58, 104, 123
Columbus, Diego, 104
Comer Hill, 58
Creoles (Criollos), 46
Crops, see Agriculture
Cuba
  art, 70
  Batista, Fulgencio, 70–71, 72

Castro, Fidel, 4, 71–77
culture, 70
economy, 47, 70–71, 72, 75
education, 75–76, 77
ethnic composition, 66, 75
geography, 64, 66
government, 64, 66, 69–77
history, 2, 3, 66–69
La Habana, 6, 39, 66, 67, 68, 71, 75
literature, 70
music, 70
natural resources, 5, 64
Spanish-American War, 68
sports, 76
tourism, 66, 70–71
U.S. involvement, 2, 3, 67, 68
U.S.S.R. involvement, 3, 74
Culture, see Art; Carnival; Dancing, Folklore; Food; Literature; Music; Religion
Curaçao, 132, 133–36, 142. See also Netherlands Antilles

Dancing, 24
  calenda, 22–23
  limbo, 184–86
  merengue, 107
  pukkumina, 26
  tambú, 136
Dessalines, Jean Jacques, 97
Destruction of the West Indies, 36
Diamond Rock, 45
Diseases, 11, 68–69
  protein malnutrition, 13
Dominica, 164–66
Dominican Republic
  art, 107
  education, 103, 106–7
  ethnic composition, 102
  food specialties, 105
  geography, 102, 103, 108
  government, 4, 103, 109–12
  -Haiti relations, 100, 102
  history, 102, 103–4, 107–9
  language, 102
  literature, 108
  natural resources, 103
  population, 102

INDEX 205

Dominican Republic *(cont.)*
religion, 107
Santiago, 105
Santo Domingo, 33, 103–5, 109
Sosúa, 106
sports, 107
Trujillo, Rafael, 109–10
U.S. involvement, 2–3, 109, 110–12
Drake, Sir Francis, 39–40, 41, 115
"Duppies" (ghosts), 85
Dutch Leewards, *see* Aruba; Bonaire; Curaçao
Dutch Windwards, *see* Saba; Sint Maarten; Statia
Duvalier, François (Papa Doc), 100–1
Duvalier, Jean Claude, 101

Economy
pre-20th-century, 11, 37–38
20th-century, 5, 13, 193–96
see also Agriculture; specific islands
Education, 17–18. *See also* specific islands
Eleuthera, 58
Employment, *see* Economy
English colonization, *see* history of specific islands
English Harbour (Antigua), 149
Enriquillo, 107–8
Ethnic composition, 5, 46. *See also* specific islands
Exports, *see* Economy
Exuma islands, 58–59

Federation of the West Indies, 83
Folklore, 23
"duppies," 85
Food specialties, 19–20
Barbados, 174
Curaçao, 134–35
Dominica, 165
Dominican Republic, 105
Jamaica, 84
Puerto Rico, 115
St. Thomas, 126
Fort de France (Martinique), 160–61

Fort Navidad, 31
Freeport (Grand Bahama), 58
French colonization, *see* history of specific islands
French West Indies, *see* Guadeloupe; Martinique
Frenchman's Cove, 88

Gambling, Grand Bahama Island, 62
Garvey, Marcus, 85–86
Geography, 3, 5–8
map, x–xi
see also specific islands
Gordon, George, 81
Gottschalk, Louis, 23
Government, 4, 5, 196. *See also* specific islands
Grand Bahama Island, 58
gambling, 62
Grand Terre, 157, 158
Grand Turk, 63
Great Abaco, 58
Great Inagua Island, 58
Greater Antilles, 3–4. *See also* specific islands
Grenada, 164, 170, 171–72
Grenadines, 169–70
Guadeloupe
Basse Terre, 159
Carnival, 157
dependencies, 159–60
economy, 153, 156
ethnic composition, 154
French influence, 156–57
geography, 153, 157, 158–59
history, 49, 154
language, 156
Pointe-à-Pitre, 157–58
Guevara, Ernesto "Che," 72, 74
Gustavia (St. Barthélemy), 160

Haiti
agriculture, 91
art, 93–95
-Dominican Republic relations, 100, 102
economy, 91, 92
education, 18, 91

206 HELLO, WEST INDIES

Haiti *(cont.)*
geography, 92
government, 4, 91, 97–101
history, 52, 96–100
language, 91
music, 92
Port-au-Prince, 92–93
religion, 89–91, 94
tourism, 95–96
U.S. intervention, 98
voodoo, 89–91, 94
Hamilton, Alexander, 2, 147
Havana (Cuba), *see* La Habana
Hawkins, John, 39, 41
Heredia, José Mariá, 67
Heyn, Piet, 41
Hippolyte, Hector, 93–94
Hispaniola, 3–4. *See also* Domini-
can Republic; Haiti
History, *see* Colonization; Piracy;
Plantocracy; specific islands
Hosein, 186–87
Housing, 13–16, 33
chattel houses, 176
haciendas, 46–47, 50
slums, 17
see also specific cities
Hurricanes, 8–9

Iles des Saintes, 159
Battle of the, 44
Indians, 11. *See also* Arawak In-
dians; Carib Indians
Industrialization, 5. *See also* econo-
my of specific islands
Institute of Puerto Rican Culture,
121

Jamaica
agriculture, 80, 86–87
economy, 5, 80, 86
education, 86
ethnic composition, 78
fauna, 80
food specialties, 84
geography, 78
government, 78, 83
history, 42, 78, 80–82, 83
Kingston, 81, 82–83
literature, 84

population, 78, 81
Port Royal, 43, 82
religion, 84–85
sports, 87
Spanish Town, 82
superstitions, 85
tourism, 78–80, 88
writers, 84
Josephine, Empress (Marie Rose
Josephine Tascher de la Pagerie), 160, 161

Kingston (Jamaica), 81, 82–83
Kingstown (St. Vincent), 168–69

La Désirade, 159
La Habana (Cuba), 6, 39, 66, 67,
68, 71, 75
Language, 4, 21. *See also* specific
islands
Las Casas, Bartolomè de, 36
Leclerc, Gen. Charles, 97
Leclerc, François, 39
Leeward Islands
definition of, 6–8
Dutch, *see* Aruba; Bonaire;
Curaçao
English-speaking, *see* Anguilla;
Antigua; Montserrat; Nevis;
St. Kitts
Lesser Antilles, 4. *See also* specific
islands
Limbo, 184–86
Literature
African folklore, 23, 85
Cuba, 70
Dominican Republic, 108
Jamaica, 84
Little Abaco, 58
L'Ollonais, François, 41
Long Island, 58
L'Ouverture, Toussaint, 96, 97

Machado, Gen. Gerardo, 70
Malaria, 11
Manley, Norman, 83
Map, x–xi
Marie-Galante, 159
Maroons, 81

INDEX 207

Martí, José, 67–68
Martinique
 Carnival, 157
 economy, 153, 156
 ethnic composition, 154
 Fort de France, 160–61
 French influence, 156–7
 geography, 153, 161
 history, 154, 160
 language, 156
 Mont Pelée, 6, 161–62
 St. Pierre, 161–62
Minerals, 5
Montserrat, 143, 151–52
Morgan, Henry, 41, 42–43
Muñoz Marín, Luis, 118–19
Muñoz Rivera, Luis, 118
Music, 22–24
 calypso, 189
 Cuba, 70
 Curaçao, 136
 Haiti, 92
 Puerto Rico, 121
 steel bands, 188–89
 Trinidad and Tobago, 188–89

Nahirs, see Arawak Indians; Carib
  Indians
Nassau (Bahama Islands), 56, 59
Natural resources, 5
Negro slaves, see Slaves, African
Nelson, Horatio, 147, 149, 177
Netherlands Antilles
 economy, 142
 geography, 132, 133
 government, 133
 history, 133
 language, 132–33
 population, 133
 see also Aruba; Bonaire; Curaçao; Saba; Sint Maarten; Statia
Nevis, 2, 143, 144, 147
New Providence, 56, 59

Obeah (black magic), 26
Oller, Francisco, 121
Operation Bootstrap (Puerto Rico),
 113–14, 119

Out Island (Bahama Islands), 56–
 59
Out Island Regatta, 58–59
Over the Hill (Nassau), 56
Oxenham, John, 40–41

Pelée, Mont, 6, 161–62
People, see Ethnic composition;
  Population
Peters, DeWitt, 93–94
Petion, Alexandre, 98
Pico Duarte, 3
Pindling, Lynden, 55, 56, 62
Piracy, 38–41, 42–43, 44
Plantocracy, 46–48, 50–52
 Jamaican, 80–81
"Platinum Coast," 176
Pointe-à-Pitre (Guadeloupe), 157–
 58
Poitier, Sidney, 56
Ponce de León, 59
Population, 5. See also specific is-
  lands
Port-au-Prince (Haiti), 92–93
Port of Spain (Trinidad), 187–88
Port Royal (Jamaica), 43, 82
Portsmouth (Dominica), 165
Privateering, see Piracy
Puerto Rico
 art, 121
 economy, 47, 113–14, 118–20
 education, 17, 122
 food specialties, 115
 geography, 113, 114
 government, 4, 113, 117–18, 119
 history, 114, 115, 117–18
 language, 115
 music, 121
 Operation Bootstrap, 113–14,
  119
 population, 113
 religion, 120–21
 San Juan, 6, 115–17
 sports, 121–22
 tourism, 114
Pukkumina, 26, 84–85

Quisqueya, 107. See also Dominican Republic

208   HELLO, WEST INDIES

Races, *see* Ethnic composition
Ras Tafarians ("Rastas"), 85
Redonda, 150
Religion, 24–26
  voodoo, 89–91, 94
  see also specific islands
Rodney, Admiral Sir George, 44
Rogers, Woodes, 44, 59
Roseau (Dominica), 165

Saba, 132, 138, 139, 140. *See also* Netherlands Antilles
Sailboating, 58–59
St. Barthélemy (St. Barts), 159–60
St. Christopher, *see* St. Kitts
St. Croix, 127–28
St. Eustatius, *see* Statia
St. George's (Grenada), 172
St. John (U.S. Virgin Islands), 127
St. John's (Antigua), 149–50
St. Kitts, 42, 143, 144–47
St. Kitts-Nevis, 143, 144. *See also* Nevis; St. Kitts
St. Lucia, 164, 166–68
St. Maarten, *see* Sint Maarten
Saint Martin, 139, 141. *See also* Sint Maarten
St. Pierre (Martinique), 161–62
St. Thomas, 125–27
St. Vincent, 168–69, 170
Saintes (Îles des Saintes), 159
  Battle of the, 44
San Juan (Puerto Rico), 6, 115–17
San Salvador, 1, 9
San Salvador Island, 58
Sans Souci, 97
Santana, Pedro, 108–9
Santiago (Dominican Republic), 105
Santo Domingo (Dominican Republic), 33, 103–5, 109
Schooling, *see* Education
Seven Years War, effect of, 44
Shango, 172
Sierra Maestra, 64
Sint Eustatius, *see* Statia

Sint Maarten, 132, 137, 138–39, 140–42. *See also* Netherlands Antilles
Slaves, African, 11–13, 50–51, 67, 81
  cultural contributions, 21, 22–24, 26
  freeing, 51–52
  housing, 14
  importing, 36, 39, 49
  rebellions, 67, 81, 96
Slaves, Indian, *see* Arawak Indians; Carib Indians
Sosúa (Dominican Republic), 106
Soufrière (village, St. Lucia), 168
Soufrière (volcano, St. Vincent), 168, 169
Spain
  colonizers from, 30–36, 37–38
  diminishing influence, 42, 68
  see also history of specific islands
Spanish-American War, 68
Spanish Town (Jamaica), 82
Sports
  Barbados, 180
  Cuba, 76
  Dominican Republic, 107
  Exuma islands, 58–59
  Jamaica, 87
  Puerto Rico, 121–22
Statia, 132, 137–38, 139–40. *See also* Netherlands Antilles
Steel bands, 188–89
Stuyvesant, Pieter, 2, 138
Sugarcane, 16–17, 48–50, 51
  Barbados, 173
  Cuba, 64, 72, 75, 77

Tainos Indians, 30
Tobago
  economy, 181, 182–83, 189–90
  education, 190–91
  ethnic composition, 183, 184, 191–92
  French influence, 184
  geography, 181
  history, 181–82, 183–84
  population, 181, 183

INDEX 209

Tobago Cays, 170
Tordesillas, Treaty of, 31
Tortola, 131
Tortuga, 42
Tourism, *see* specific islands
Toussaint l'Ouverture, 96, 97
Trade, *see* Economy
Trade wind, 6, 8
Trinidad
  African influence, 184–86
  Carnival, 181, 184, 186
  economy, 5, 181, 182–83, 188,
    189–90, 191
  education, 190–91
  ethnic composition, 183, 187,
    191–92
  fauna, 182
  festivals, 186–87
  geography, 181, 182
  government, 187, 191
  history, 33, 181–82, 183
  population, 181, 183
  Port of Spain, 187–88
  steel bands, 188–89
Trinidad and Tobago, *see* Tobago;
  Trinidad
Trujillo, Rafael Leonidas, 109–10
Turks and Caicos Islands, 63

Unemployment, *see* Economy
U.S. involvement, 2–3, 196–98. *See*
  also specific islands
U.S. Virgin Islands
  Americanization, 126
  economy, 128, 129
  education, 128
  government, 126, 129–30

history, 124–25
St. Croix, 127–28
St. John, 127
St. Thomas, 126–27
  tourism, 126–27
University of Puerto Rico, 17
University of the West Indies, 17

Villaverda, Cirilo, 67
Virgin Gorda, 131
Virgin Islands
  British, 130–31
  climate, 123
  geography, 123, 124
  history, 123–24
  population, 123
  U.S., 124–30
Virgin Islands National Park, 127
Volcanoes, 6
  Mont Pelée, 161–62
  Soufrière, 168, 169
Voodoo, 89–91, 94

Watling, *see* San Salvador
Weather, *see* Climate
Willemstad (Curaçao), 133–34,
  142
Windward Islands
  definition of, 6, 8
  Dutch, *see* Saba; Sint Maarten;
    Statia
  English-speaking, 163–172
Writers, *see* Literature

Xamayca, 78

Yellow fever, 11, 68–69

The Author

A free-lance writer, Morris Weeks has traveled widely throughout North and South America, the Caribbean Islands, Europe, and the British Isles. Although he was born in Babylon, New York, he spent his early years in La Jolla, California, and later returned to the East to attend Princeton University, where he received his A.B. degree.

Mr. Weeks' book on the West Indies, like his previous books, *Hello, Venezuela* and *Hello, Mexico*, grew out of his interest in Latin America and the Caribbean.

He now lives in the harbor town of Sea Cliff, New York, with his wife. There he pursues his great enthusiasm for sail boating, as well as his other hobbies which are as widely divergent as tennis, gardening, bridge, and playing the piano.